JOHN WYNDHAM

WRITERS AND THEIR WORK

SERIES EDITORS:

Professor Dinah Birch CBE,
University of Liverpool
Professor Dame Janet Beer,
University of Liverpool

Writers and Their Work, launched in 1994 in association with the British Council, won immediate acclaim for its publication of brief but rigorous critical examinations of the works of distinguished writers and schools of writing. The series embraces the best of modern literary theory and criticism, and features studies of many popular contemporary writers, as well as the canonical figures of literature and important literary genres.

© Copyright 2025 by David Seed

First published in 2025 by
Liverpool University Press
4 Cambridge Street
Liverpool L69 7ZU

on behalf of
Northcote House Publishers Ltd
Mary Tavy
Devon PL19 9PY

David Seed has asserted the right to be identified as the author of this book in accordance with the Copyright, Designs and Patents Act 1988. All rights reserved. No part of this book may be reproduced, stored in a retrieval system, or transmitted, in any form or by any means, electronic, mechanical, photocopying, recording, or otherwise, without the prior written permission of the publisher.

British Library Cataloguing-in-Publication Data
A catalogue record for this book is available from the British Library

ISBN 978-1-83624-354-0 (hardback)
ISBN 978-1-83624-386-1 (paperback)

Typeset by Carnegie Book Production, Lancaster

JOHN WYNDHAM

David Seed

NORTHCOTE

Contents

Biographical Outline		vii
Introduction		1
1.	Prewar	7
2.	Triffids and Other Invasions	27
3.	Permutations of Science Fiction	51
4.	*Consider Her Ways* and Other Stories	69
5.	Wyndham on SF	93
Notes		115
Bibliography		127
Appendix		147
General Index		161
Index to Wyndham's Works		168

Biographical Outline

1902/3	John Wyndham Parkes Lucas Beynon Harris born in the West Midlands village of Dorridge. His mother was Gertrude Parkes, daughter of a Birmingham ironmaster; his father was George Beynon Harris, a barrister.
1909–1911	Wyndham lived in Edgbaston, Birmingham.
1911	His parents separated.
1913	His father unsuccessfully sued for custody of his children. Wyndham was traumatized by the divorce and estranged from his father.
1914–1915	Attends Edgbaston High School for Boys.
1915	Attends Shardlow Hall school in Derbyshire and begins to read the fiction of H. G. Wells, who remained an important influence throughout his career.
1918–1921	Attends Bedales School, boarding and co-educational, in Hampshire. His earliest recorded fiction, a tribute piece to H. G. Wells called 'Vivisection', appeared in *The Bee*, the school magazine. Bedales made a lasting impression on Wyndham, and he maintained contact with the school throughout his career. Wyndham's younger brother Vivian Beynon Harris also attended Bedales.
1924	Takes up full-time residence in the Quaker-founded Penn Club, Bloomsbury. About this time his mother was admitted to a hydropathy establishment in Matlock, Derbyshire.
1925	Starts writing stories for publication.
1927	His first novel published – *The Curse of the Burdens* – a

	crime mystery as by 'John B. Harris'. His pen names were to vary until the 1950s.
1930	With 'Future Flying Fiction' wins competition for a slogan for the journal *Air Wonder Stories*.
1931	First SF story, 'Worlds to Barter', published in *Wonder Stories*. Meets wife-to-be Grace Wilson, a teacher also resident in the Penn Club.
1934	Father dies.
1935	First SF novel published: *The Secret People* set in North Africa. Crime mystery published, *Foul Play Suspected*. Probably meets George Orwell, then serving as assistant in Hampstead bookshop.
1936	Second SF novel published, *Planet Plane*, retitled *Stowaway to Mars*.
1937	Interviewed by Walter Gillings (editor) in launch number of *Scientifiction*.
1940	After outbreak of war, serves as censor for Ministry of Information.
1943	Enlists in the army.
1944	Becomes cypher operator in Royal Corps of Signals. Participates in Normandy campaign and maintains extensive correspondence with Grace Wilson.
1948–1951	Brother Vivian publishes four novels: *Trouble at Hanard* and *Confusion at Camden Rig* (both 1948), *One Thing Constant* (1949) and *Song to a Siren* (1951). Encourages Wyndham to restart writing.
1948.	Writes novel about Nazi resurgence, *Fury of Creation* later retitled *Plan for Chaos* (published 2009). First story, 'The Eternal Eve', published as by 'John Wyndham'. Nova Publications formed by John Carnell and Walter Gillings, with Wyndham topping the list of subscribers.
1949	Reads Orwell's *Nineteen Eighty-Four* soon after publication.
1949–1953	SF journal *New Worlds* launched under the editorship of John Carnell.
1950	SF author Frederik Pohl becomes Wyndham's US literary agent. Wyndham planning a *Fury of Creation* trilogy to include *Plan for Chaos*, *The Day of the Triffids*, and *The Chrysalids*.

BIOGRAPHICAL OUTLINE

1951	*The Day of the Triffids* published. Abridged serialization as 'Revolt of the Triffids' in *Collier's*.
1952	Lunches with Fulbright Fellow (later bibliographer) E. F. Bleiler, who secures for him a copy of the Dutch plagiarized edition of *Triffids*.
1953	*The Kraken Wakes* published. US title *Out of the Deeps*, abbreviated and altered. Mother dies. Supplies brief biographical note for Penguin where he 'decided to try a modified form of what is unhappily known as "science fiction"'.
1954	*Jizzle* (stories) published. Contributes editorial 'The Pattern of Science Fiction' to *Science-Fantasy* 3 (Spring). Gives talk on escapism to the English-Speaking Union.
1955	*The Chrysalids* published; US title *Re-Birth*. Edits *The Best from 'New Worlds' Science Fiction* (T. V. Boardman), with introduction by Wyndham and foreword by John Carnell.
1956	*The Sands of Time* published. Five short stories and five novelettes with a foreword by Wyndham.
1957	*The Midwich Cuckoos* published. The 15th World Science Fiction Convention held at King's Court Hotel, London. As president, Wyndham presents Hugo Awards to John W. Campbell, Carnell and John Victor Peterson. US collection of stories published: *Tales of Gooseflesh and Laughter*. Interviewed by Keith Waterhouse for *Daily Mirror*.
1958–1959	Replies to questions from Kinglsey Amis on SF for *New Maps of Hell*.
1959	*The Outward Urge* published. A fix-up novel with four chapters, a fifth added in 1961, as by Wyndham and Lucas Parkes (one of Wyndham's pseudonyms). Receives Infinity Award from *Infinity Science Fiction* for *Sometime, Never* (1966), containing 'Consider Her Ways' and stories by William Golding and Mervyn Peake.
1960	*Trouble with Lichen* published. Interview with Derek Hart on *Tonight*, BBC TV, 6 September. Kingsley Amis's *New Maps of Hell* published and reviewed by Wyndham in *John O'London's*.

1961	MGM releases *The Village of the Damned*, based on *The Midwich Cuckoos* and followed by a 1964 sequel *Children of the Damned*. *Consider Her Ways and Others* (stories) published; US title *The Infinite Moment*. 'Jizzle' filmed as 'Maria' for series 'Alfred Hitchcock Presents'. Invited by Hitchcock to write film script for Daphne Du Maurier's *The Birds*. Declined.
1962	Contributes to BBC Radio programme *The Realm of Perhaps*. Participants include Brian Aldiss, J. G. Ballard and John Brunner.
1963	Marries Grace Wilson. They move to a house in Steep, Hampshire, near to Bedales School. Security Pictures release film of *The Day of the Triffids*.
1964	'Consider Her Ways' broadcast on 'The Alfred Hitchcock Hour'.
1966	Approached by *The Weekend Telegraph* and *The News of the World* to participate in celebrating the centenary of H. G. Wells's birth. Contributes to discussion about Wells on BBC Home Service.
1968	*Chocky* published. Last story to be published in his lifetime, 'A Life Postponed' in *Galaxy Science Fiction*.
1969	Dies of heart attack.
1979	*Web* published.

Introduction

John Wyndham Parkes Lucas Beynon Harris (1903–69), usually known as John Wyndham, was a formative figure in the postwar evolution of British science fiction, producing a series of understated narratives usually dramatizing the blind forces of Nature. He spent much of his youth in Birmingham, becoming estranged from his father after his parents separated in 1911. Wyndham then attended a number of schools, notably Bedales in Hampshire, where he first tried his hand at writing. Also in the 1910s he discovered the science fiction of H. G. Wells, who was to remain an important influence, especially in embedding scientific speculation within contemporary society (see Priest 2000). At the end of the First World War Wyndham took up residence in the Penn Club for private members, founded by the Quakers in 1920. The property was in Bloomsbury, close to the British Museum and Senate House, where he stayed for the next 30 years. In her 2019 biography, *Hidden Wyndham*, Amy Binns stresses how private an individual he was, as reflected in the very few interviews he ever gave and the few photographs available of him.

Wyndham's younger brother, Vivian Beynon Harris (1906–87), accompanied him to Bedales school and during the 1920s had a brief career in acting. After the Second World War he published four novels, just at the point where Wyndham was looking to revive his own career. Vivian later described these novels as 'time-passers and laugh providers', never really considering a career as a writer for himself, partly because he suffered from ill health.[1]

The two brothers stayed in regular contact and soon after Wyndham's death Vivian planned to write a biography to be called *Jack and Me: Growing Up with John Wyndham*. In the event, he never got beyond the opening stage of this project, which, now published, gives us valuable commentary on the Wyndham family and on the writer's career. From him we learn that Wyndham was a voracious reader and started writing at the age of 12. Perhaps in compensation for the early disruptions in family life, Wyndham found a long-standing home in the Penn Club, where he lived with his partner (later wife) Grace Wilson in adjoining rooms. Vivian explains the attractions of the club as follows: 'First he met distinguished and educated [?minds] and there were always members to talk with [...] Also he was a very curious person and whenever he came to stay with us he would always wander round peering into cupboards and hidey-holes to see what was inside'.[2] Vivian also recorded his brother's strong sense of privacy, stressing that he 'did not like the communication media. At least, he didn't like appearing on them'. In Wyndham's obituary notice for *The Times*, probably written by Vivian, the same point is made that he was a 'shy, retiring man, with a great dislike of personal publicity'.[3] From the same source we also learn that Wyndham was an enthusiastic supporter of the National Trust. He married in 1963 and spent his last years in a country house near Petersfield, Hampshire, significantly also near to Bedales School, whose events he also supported long after he had left it.

In 1927, Wyndham published his first novel, *The Curse of the Burdens*, a complex country house thriller, but shortly afterwards discovered science fiction through magazines like *Amazing Stories*. In 1931 he published his first story in that field, 'Worlds to Barter'. Subsequently he continued to publish stories, mainly science fiction, in Britain and the USA, from the very beginning trying to differentiate his fiction from the more lurid and sensational space adventures known as 'pulp science fiction'. Although for much of his career he remained dissatisfied with the label 'science fiction', Wyndham constantly tried to differentiate British practice from American, and particularly after the war he combined a critical discussion of the genre with book reviewing. This will be discussed in Chapter 5, and the Appendix reprints for the first time his 1955 essay 'Science-Fiction: Space-Opera', one of his most considered pieces. Here he examines the pedigree of science fiction, draws distinctions between European and American practice, contrasts space opera with more serious fiction, and recommends contemporary authors like Aldous Huxley (*Ape and Essence*), Ward Moore and Kurt Vonnegut.

1950 marked a turning point for Wyndham in that *Collier's*, a leading US general interest magazine, bought the serial rights to *The Day of the Triffids*, which was also accepted for UK book publication, appearing in 1951. At the same time Wyndham adopted his main pen name, explaining it as follows to his then agent, the US SF novelist Frederik Pohl: 'The original idea of John Wyndham was that I was using it for a different style of stuff'. It was 'not cluttered up with memories of early Wonder Stories'.[4] In other words it signalled an attempt by Wyndham to distance himself from his pre-war writing with its connections with pulp. A further important development followed when Penguin Books published a paperback edition of *The Day of the Triffids* in 1954. The editorial preamble to the novel declared that it was 'one of the very few books of its kind that can stand comparison with [...] the astonishing science-novels of H. G. Wells' and went on to stress its methodical plausibility. The avoidance of the science fiction label is of its time, but the publication signals Wyndham's entry into the literary mainstream, and Penguin Books subsequently became his main publisher.

The Day of the Triffids marked the beginning of Wyndham's major period of productivity throughout the 1950s. His account of the species battle between humanity and peripatetic predatory plants was followed in 1953 by *The Kraken Wakes* (US title *Out of the Deeps*), where mysterious creatures from the ocean depths prey on humans, and in 1955 by *The Chrysalids* (US title *Re-Birth*) set in a future Canada in the wake of an atomic war. *The Midwich Cuckoos* (1957) returned the action to a contemporary English village when a mysterious seizure induces mass pregnancies. *The Outward Urge* (1959) is a fix-up novel assembled from stories which give Wyndham's unusual take on interplanetary travel, and *Trouble with Lichen* (1960) explores the cultural upheavals triggered by the discovery of an anti-ageing substance. In most of these works Wyndham embeds the action in contemporary Britain, implicitly drawing on recent memories of the war to evoke crises of survival. As the publicity machine swung into action with these successes, Wyndham confided to Frederik

Pohl 'I hate having my photograph taken' and his reclusive nature was subsequently examined in the 2005 BBC TV film *John Wyndham: The Invisible Man of Science Fiction*.[5]

Between 1955 and 1970, the crime writer Edmund Crispin edited seven anthologies with the title *Best SF* published by the mainstream Faber and Faber. Three stories by Wyndham appeared in these collections, including the 1955 volume, where Crispin defined a science-fiction story as 'one which presupposes a technology, or an effect of a technology, or a disturbance in the natural order, such as humanity, up to the time of writing, has not in actual fact experienced'.[6] Wyndham was so impressed by this definition that he quoted it in the opening of his 1955 Appendix article and in his foreword to his 1956 story collection *The Seeds of Time*.

During the 1950s Wyndham became a central figure in the establishment of science fiction within the cultural mainstream of Great Britain. This was helped by his contributions to journals like *New Worlds*, whose editor John Carnell in 1957 organized the 15th World Science Fiction Convention in London, where Wyndham served as president of the convention committee.[7] His role included introducing the guest of honour John W. Campbell. He invited Ray Bradbury, whose *The Silver Locusts* (the UK title of *The Martian Chronicles*) he valued, but Bradbury was unable to attend. Another convention organizer was Wyndham's friend from before the war, Arthur C. Clarke, whose fiction he knew and respected. Clarke for his part later described *The Day of the Triffids* as an 'immortal story'.[8]

By 1960 Wyndham could be introduced on the BBC TV programme *Tonight* as 'one of the country's best-known writers of science fiction'. In an interview opened with brief readings from *The Kraken Wakes* and *The Day of the Triffids*, Derek Hart asked Wyndham how he devised his subjects, which received the following answer: 'what one starts with is the theme and then you work it out to the logical conclusion as far as possible'.[9] Wyndham went on to add that he had to consider upper and lower limits to his subjects, citing the examples of spaceships which were more acceptable in the USA than Britain, and the mutations in *The Chrysalids* which, if they were excessive, might distract from the narrative. Two years later Wyndham, along with Kingsley Amis,

Brian Aldiss, J. G. Ballard and others, participated in *The Realm of Perhaps*, a radio discussion of science fiction.[10]

The programmes featuring Wyndham formed part of a BBC investigation of the possibilities for science fiction drama, which resulted in *Out of the Unknown*, four series running from 1965 to 1971. Series 1 opened with Wyndham's 'No Place Like Earth', a combination of 'Time to Rest and 'No Place Like Earth' run into a single work. Earlier in that decade, in 1962, ABC TV had started a similar series called *Out of This World* which used Wyndham's 'Dumb Martian' on 'Armchair Theatre' as a launch event. These series formed part of a broader impetus to produce science fiction films which included those centring on Nigel Kneale's Professor Quatermass (named in his last essay by Wyndham), the *A for Andromeda* serial from 1961 written by the astronomer Fred Hoyle (famous for his 1957 novel *The Black Cloud*) and the launch in 1963 of the BBC TV series about a character displaced in space and time, *Doctor Who*.

Wyndham's fiction has constantly been adapted for the media, particularly for radio drama, television and film. One of the most famous was *Village of the Damned* (1960) from *The Midwich Cuckoos*, which was originally planned for US production and then moved to the UK. Its hallmark image was the glowing eyes of the blonde-haired children, which, Wyndham admitted, made them seem much more evil than in the novel. After further film adaptations in 1964 and 1995, a 2022 TV serial restored Wyndham's original title. In 1962 the first adaptation of *The Day of the Triffids* was released, which diverged from the novel in removing the character Josella, broadening out the setting to continental Europe, and having an anti-climactic conclusion in showing that the triffids could be combatted with salt water. Television adaptations followed in 1981 and 2009. Since then, movie adaptations of Wyndham's works have continued to be made, all with their different revisions of scene and action.[11]

1961 saw the publication of one of the first critical studies of science fiction. Kingsley Amis's *New Maps of Hell* was triggered by his teaching at Princeton University and combines a survey of the field with an attempt at definition of the genre through a hypothetical innovation. Wyndham's novella 'Consider Her Ways' is discussed within the context of utopian fiction but it should be noted here that Amis had already paid a tribute to Wyndham in his fulsome review of *Trouble with Lichen*, where he declared: 'if even a tenth of science fiction were as good, we should be in clover'.[12] Wyndham in effect returned the compliment in his review of *New Maps of Hell*, where he quoted with approval Amis's description of science fiction as a 'means of dramatizing social inquiry' and claims to share his perception that 'never was a well-intentioned genre more bedevilled by a smirched label and a monstrous percentage of dross'.[13] The dross in question refers particularly to pre-war science fiction stories; now Wyndham is gradually recognizing the emergence of valuable new practitioners in the field.

In his 1983 history of the New Wave in science fiction, *The Entropy Exhibition*, the UK novelist Colin Greenland leads off with a discussion of *The Midwich Cuckoos* in relation to the generation gap, and the steady growth of subsequent Wyndham criticism has explored his engagement with national values and the cultural complexities of the Cold War, despite Brian Aldiss's notorious thumbnail description of Wyndham as the 'master of the cosy catastrophe'.[14] Along with this growth in critical attention, Wyndham has also been receiving recognition from such contemporary novelists as Stephen King (who described Wyndham as 'perhaps the best writer of science fiction that England has ever produced'), Margaret Atwood and Jeff VanderMeer.[15]

In 1998 the John Wyndham Archive was acquired by Liverpool University and since then has been housed in their Special Collections.[16]

***

Note: Unless otherwise indicated, page references throughout will be to the latest Penguin editions of Wyndham's works.

1

Prewar

Wyndham's earliest published work of fiction appeared in *The Bee*, the magazine of Bedales boarding school, in 1919. Clearly drawing on *The Island of Doctor Moreau* (1896), 'Vivisection' presents the diary narrative of an Oxford science graduate who has been following the experiments and 'wild' ideas of one Professor Langley. Wyndham transposes these experiments from the Pacific to a Dartmoor estate which the narrator Lunst visits to his cost. In the night he hears a confusion of cries from animals and possibly a human. As the sounds approach, he turns on his light, with the following revelation: 'I saw before me not a pony, but two beings with the hindquarters of a goat, and the top part bearing a strong resemblance to a man'.[1] Returning later to his room, he discovers the role of housemaids being played by 'two little creatures about four feet high, with black faces and curly hair'. In the grounds he is even more mystified by being confronted by a strange tall figure with short legs who speaks to him, answering his questions cryptically with 'The Master'. The story is essentially a sketch which, like Wells's original, plays on disproportion and which replaces night-time horrors with daytime scrutiny, inviting the reader to speculate on what possible experiments might have led to these results.

Wyndham explicitly returned to *Doctor Moreau* in his 1933 story 'The Perfect Creature', which describes a scientist's attempt to create new creatures in an English village. One character suspects him of being a 'super-vivisectionist' like Wells's character, but the reality proves to be more complex. Spurred on by his discovery of a 'life-force', the scientist has been experimenting with redesigning the human form and incorporating steel supports into the body. The 'perfect creature' is finally revealed as a grotesque hybrid of limbs and geometrical shapes, ironically named Una after the character in Spenser's *Faerie Queen*. 'She' disappears in the chaos of the final scene and shows how Wyndham was engaging in a subject dialogue with Wells. Wyndham's story is also an exercise in relocation and gives us an early example of his evolving technique of embedding the extraordinary within the details of English social life.

Wyndham's first adult contact with science fiction came in 1930 when he won a competition for the best slogan ('Future Flying Fiction') to be applied to Hugo Gernsback's magazine *Air Wonder Stories*. Despite his success, the slogan was never applied because that same year the magazine merged with Gernsback's *Wonder Stories*, one of the main American outlets for science fiction in the early 1930s. Subtitled *The Magazine of Prophetic Fiction*, its pages carried numerous advertisements for electrical goods and regular factual pieces on science. The first issues to carry stories by Wyndham in May 1931 and 1932, for example, carried essays by Gernsback on telepathy and 'The Wonders of Atomic Power'.[2] The latter's brief was educational, promoting inventions and predictive. In March 1933 he reflected on this fiction's evocation of technological change and declared that 'everything that the machine age has to offer, many of the possibilities arising from the reign of the machine, have been anticipated by authors of science fiction for many years'.[3] The emphasis in *Wonder Stories* on technological progress was matched by the frequent appearance of stories about hostile species and travel through space and time. As John Cheng has shown, by popularizing such terms as 'amazing' and 'wonder', Gernsback's publications 'gave a distinctively modern articulation of science, linking knowledge, change, and progress'.[4] This was the context Wyndham entered with his first SF stories.

Throughout the 1930s, Wyndham was forming a largely negative impression of American science fiction stories, which he later described as 'ingenious, slick, mechanical, careful in argument, careless in style, and considerably weakened in holding power by lack of attention to the humanities' (see Appendix). There were exceptions, however. In the early 1930s, David Lasser, the managing editor of *Wonder Stories*, was calling for greater realism from his writers. He rejected space opera in favour of narrative specificity, continuing that 'the "modern" science story should not try to be a world-sweeping epic. It should rather try to portray *intensively* some particular phase of our future civilization'.[5]

In 1937, Walter Gillings's UK fanzine *Scientifiction* (whose title applied a 1915 Gernsback coinage) ran an article called 'What "S.F". Means in U.S'. which argued that it specialized in fantastic adventure narratives centring on figures like Buck Rogers and Flash Gordon.[6] Wyndham followed a similar line with a more challenging title in the same issue – 'Why This Cosmic Wild West Stuff?' – where he declared that the reason he 'first read scientifiction was not solely for the sensation of the moment, but because it left me with something to think about when the tale was finished'. Accordingly he argued that the British SF reader had different expectations: 'He wants better explanations, which he can believe, and he can't be spoofed quite so easily'.[7] The evolution of his thinking about science fiction will be examined in Chapter 5.

Between 1931 and 1934, Wyndham contributed nine pieces to *Wonder Stories*. His first story, 'Worlds to Barter' (May 1931) continues his serial engagement with Wells's fiction and features a number of characteristics which were to recur in his other stories. The subject is introduced by embedding the reader in a scientific experiment (in the year 1945) where the narrator is assisting a scientist called Professor Lestrange.[8] Where the experiment raises our expectation of departure from the present, Wyndham reverses this by having a figure from the twenty-second century arrive in a machine resembling the 'skeleton framework of a miniature building', constructed of 'bright silvery bars', who proceeds to take over the narration. This early example of framing includes an explicit rejection of linear progress when we are told that his future 'would have disappointed Wells and his fellow prophets to have had a true vision of A.D. 2145' since technology had slowed down by that century.[9] More ominously, the world of the future is being threatened by a race which declares: 'we have conquered that we may gain the Earth'. In a meeting with these beings from the far future, the latter are described as 'stunted, malformed, hairless, toothless and deaf', but technologically so advanced that they easily impose their will on the future Earth.[10] The confrontation is so severe that it poses a Darwinian challenge to the listeners of the 'survival of the mentally fittest' and humans are dismissed as mere 'savages'. Although there is a return to relative normality at the end of the story, Wyndham still leaves ominous implications open for the future, another characteristic of his stories to come.

Unlike *The Time Machine* (1895), in 'Worlds to Barter' time travel has already been invented and the stranger engages in a lively dialogue with the professor about his own future discoveries. In short, this dialogue questions the theorizing and implementation of the professor's experiment and establishes a situation of ignorance even shared by the newcomer, who proceeds to criticize the others' perception of time: 'Because I am here now, I know that time is somehow folded or circular so that it is all co-existent, or non-existent. But of the working principle of that machine which brought me here, I am as ignorant as you'.[11] Having questioned the linear conception of evolution, he explicitly references *When the Sleeper Wakes* (1899) in order to make clear that we are certainly not going to get a rerun of Wells. Technical progress does take place thanks mainly to Professor Lestrange's battery, of which he himself at that stage knows nothing, but external threats loom when the people of 2134 glimpse their own 'remote descendants' when they discover a mysterious corpse. The latter is still visibly human but carries the features outlined by Wells in his 1893 sketch of 'The Man of the Year Million', where his Professor Holzkopf (Wood-Head) states: 'the coming man [...] will clearly have a larger brain and a slighter body than the present'.[12]

In one sense Wyndham is moving well away from any reassuring model of constant evolutionary improvement. In another, he complicates prediction by having a human from the near future himself serve as a witness of threat from the five thousand and twentieth century, when a disembodied voice warns his contemporaries that they have a stark choice facing them: either 'elimination' or submission to the will of the future-dwellers. The latter make an initial appeal to reason by gathering diplomats in a 'silver cylinder' and flying them to the Sahara, a setting which would play a major role in Wyndham's 1935 novel *The Secret People*, discussed below. Nothing comes of that project and multiple transporters appear in western cities to deport willing citizens. Despite the ostensible appeal to reason, these events suggest the sheer power of the aggressor's will. Again, following orders from on high, all these events are recorded on film, scenes fading in and out of visibility as if the humans have become the helpless spectators of their fate, and the story ends abruptly when the professor and his companions manage to return to his laboratory. There is a notional relief in this return but of course one hugely overshadowed by the ominous post-narrative.

Stories like these share Wyndham's indifference to technological detail, which can also be witnessed in his 1932 story 'The Venus Adventure'. This too appeared in *Wonder Stories* with an editorial gloss explaining that its subject is 'the effect of environment upon two races: the rise of one and the steady degeneration of another to almost the level of the brute'.[13] In fact the main ironies are directed against religion in its construction of beliefs out of a story of origins added to a 'set of customs and superstitions'.[14] A Scottish Puritan forms a sect with the slogan 'what's natural's right' but collaborates with a scientist to fly to Venus. Wyndham gives very little information about how this is managed or how a later group from Earth manage the same journey. Suffice it that over the intervening centuries the human settlers have either regressed towards bestiality or evolved through their development of scientific analysis. In contrast with the expectations aroused by the title, Venus is used to set up a displaced parable on the human capacity for reason.

In 'Wanderers of Time' (1933) we return to the subject of time travel, once again presented quite differently from Wells. Set in the countryside near Chicago, the narrative describes the sudden appearance of a 'glittering cylinder' to the astonishment of a passer-by.[15] We scarcely register an impression of technological innovation and possible weaponry before a panel in the machine opens to reveal another human, the first time-traveller who has been searching for his disappeared lover. As usual, Wyndham focuses on the unexpected aspects of time travel rather than its technology. Fleeing from an unwelcome encounter with the local police, the cylinder travels into time again, this time encountering on landing yet another machine which resembles a 'cubical cage with six-foot sides'.[16] Of course every device must have its pilot, and the newcomer (called Del), is fortunately fluent enough in English to explain that he has come from the far future, but that his device has malfunctioned like the original cylinder. Del performs the role of commentator, advising the others how to behave when they are taken captive by a group of threatening red machines. While in captivity they meet other human time travellers who have met the same fate and it is Del who points out that the creators of the machines are none other than ants, but without explaining how this came about. By this point the subject of time travel has proliferated, has shifted away from efficient experiment through malfunction, and bleakly evoked a far future where an alien species appears to have power over humans.

In this story Wyndham downplays the drama of time travel by showing how unpredictable the vehicles are and therefore how little control technicians have over their inventions. A similar spirit informs 'The Third Vibrator' (1933), which frames its subject through a scientist who has been confined in a mental asylum. He takes over the narrative and claims to have devised a super-weapon which 'has ended war'. Now the location segues away from a recognizable present to the mythical continents of Lemuria and Atlantis, both containing figures who claim to have perfected the perfect weapon. But both are revealed to have their faults, and the story returns to the first scientist, whose pathology is confirmed as a self-delusive dream.

Far from opening up new possibilities, space travel in these stories is shown to reveal unforeseen dangers. 'Invisible Monster' (1933), for example, describes the return to Earth of a spaceship carrying a huge, invisible creature which presents a deadly threat to any humans near it. 'The Man from Earth' (1934) plays far more effectively with the reader's reactions in establishing a setting on Venus where a mysterious valley is explored and traces of primeval creatures presented in a kind of natural museum. One cage, however, holds a 'solitary, curious creature which stood erect upon hind legs'.[17] It is of course a human being. Wyndham has reversed our perspective to present the human as alien. This is only part of the subject, however. As the human starts communicating with the Venusians, he explains that space travel has become a commercial enterprise on Earth, the subject of competition between two industrial complexes, the one clearly modelled on Imperial Chemical Industries (ICI), founded in 1926.

Just as these companies see space exploration as a means

of expanding their empire, a new species of plant can be used to further imperialism on Earth. This is the subject of 'The Puff-Ball Menace' (1933), which experiments with the subject of species predation which Wyndham was to develop in *The Day of the Triffids* (see Chapter 2). The story is explicitly framed as an ironic criticism of the logic of empire, the principle that 'might is right'.[18] A biologist in the country of Ghangistan devises a plant which will multiply indefinitely, and which is fatal to humans. We then cut to Cornwall where a young man is enjoying his leave from Amalgamated Chemicals, yet another possible allusion to ICI. He is shown a strange plant, 'a ball of blotchy, virulent yellow' which has been sent to England by 'agents' of Experimental Growers.[19] Identified as a hybrid fungus, this plant proliferates dramatically, producing a rash on humans and threatening other plant species. The central core of the story focuses on the slowness of the authorities to recognize the danger and to take measures. Eventually the army is brought in and the area cordoned off, but the plot fails from an undetected weakness in the biological make-up of the plant whereby it morphs to harmless normality. Wyndham clearly sets the story up as an ironic parable of empire and when he returns the narrative to Ghangistan in the coda, the prince denies closure to the ending by reflecting that 'there are other means'.[20] In other words, the threat to empire persists.

Empire also informs Wyndham's first SF novel which was published in 1935. *The Secret People* (originally called *Sub-Sahara*) was serialized in Odham's weekly magazine *The Passing Show*, which was an important British science fiction outlet in the early 1930s. It carried the serial of Edward Balmer and Philip Wylie's *When Worlds Collide* (1934–5) and also Edgar Rice Burroughs's *Lost on Venus* and *Pirates of Venus* (1934). *The Secret People* is a futuristic adventure story, set in the year 1964, describing how a British pilot called Mark Sunnet and his companion Margaret survive after their rocket-plane crashes in an inland sea in North Africa. They discover a whole network of caves populated by a mysterious race they never even knew existed. Most of the narrative describes Mark's experiences with other human captives who have fallen into the clutches of the cave-dwellers until he and, quite separately his companion Margaret, effect their escape and return to civilization.

In his preamble Wyndham establishes cultural links with the Europe of the 1930s. Mark pilots a rocket-plane, which was the subject of experiments by Fritz von Opel in Germany and the first public flight took place in 1929. *The Secret People* opens dramatically with a silver plane roaring over the Algerian landscape on a flight from Paris, an image which encapsulates the colonial associations of the latest European technology. A second image reinforces these links when the plane passes over the 'New Sea', a recent construct in the 'shotts' or inland depressions fed by massive pumps in the Tunisian port of Gabes. Wyndham may have taken this concept from Verne's novel *Invasion of the Sea* (1905), part-serialized in English in 1908, which was set in the 1930s and which dramatized the efforts by engineers with a French military escort to construct this sea. The project had a historical base in the 1870s when Francois Loudaire and Ferdinand De Lesseps, the architect of the Suez Canal named in the text by Wyndham, formulated such a plan. The construction has been agreed by France and Italy, the main colonizers of North Africa in this period.[21]

The narrative proper of *The Secret People* begins when the plane crashes, floats briefly on the surface, and then sinks into subterranean cavern, where Mark and his companion find themselves in a labyrinth of passages. These passages are lit throughout, which suggests human habitation, hence the subtitle of the serial 'Prisoner Under the Sea'. A key moment comes when Mark realizes that he is being watched by a short figure with 'grey-white' skin and 'large, black eyes'. Here Wyndham is drawing partly on the Morlocks in Wells's *The Time Machine*, who are also 'grey-white', short in stature, with large eyes. Like Wells's scientist, Mark passes out when attacked by hundreds of these 'pygmies', as they are called throughout the novel, and his captivity begins.

Unlike the Morlocks, the cave-dwellers are never named and are mainly evoked as an anonymous undifferentiated racial underclass. Their enigmatic status is reflected in the fact that they have constructed a lighting system, but their knowledge of technology is never specified. Also they seem to have an artistic sense as revealed by their paintings on the cave walls, but these too remain unexplained. Through conversations with the other captives Mark learns a little about the behaviour of the creatures referred to variously as dwarfs, gnomes or pygmies; but that information serves mainly to set up his plans to escape. In a situation which locally inverts the assumed racial hierarchy, he discovers that the captives include not only Whites but also Arabs, Negroes and Indians, who have all proved unable to outwit the cave-dwellers.

At the same moment when he discovers the pygmies' existence, Mark also realizes that some caves are full of giant mushrooms. Wyndham took this notion of a 'fungus forest' from John Uri Lloyd's 1897 hollow earth narrative *Etidorhpa*, with the difference that the latter is introduced during subterranean exploration and with the suggestion that these vegetables might be mind-altering when consumed. In *The Secret People*, the Darwinian emphasis on survival means that these mushrooms must be used as weapons whereby their puff-balls can emit spores to blind enemies.

Our perception of the cave-dwellers is complicated by the narrative strand focusing on Margaret, who remains isolated among them. Because she has acquired a cat named Bast, after the Egyptian goddess, the pygmies treat her with respect and she develops an intellectual relationship with one of their wise men named Garm, this time echoing that of a Norse dog or wolf in mythology. This character, however, doesn't soften the 'othering' of the pygmies because Wyndham stresses how untypical he is of his race. His role is to facilitate a running dialogue with Margaret about the cave-dwellers from their point of view. With convenient speed she learns their language and engages in a dialogue with Garm about which creatures have souls and what it means to worship a god. These chapters are clearly designed to balance Mark's discussion of his captors with a self-styled anthropologist called Gordon, who explains how 'the dominant races pursued their appointed course on the surface; the memory of the pygmies grew fainter until, at last, it was entirely rubbed away, and they were forgotten, lost' (111). Just as they are driven by the impulse to survive, so the novel's plot concludes with Mark and Margaret returning to civilization.

Although Wyndham was to deal at length with the red planet in his 1936 novel *Stowaway to Mars*, he had earlier engaged with the subject in 'The Lost Machine' (1932), subsequently incorporated into the novel through the story of Joan. Here he experiments with perspective reversal in framing an account by a sentient machine from Mars which crashes on Earth. Conveniently gifted with telepathy and linguistic skills, the machine reverses the standard pattern of the alien encounter narrative, pausing to exclaim at one point: 'men afraid of a machine'.[22] The traditional signs of technological and military progress are presented as startlingly primitive. An episode in a circus blurs the distinction between humans and animals. Brief personal interaction with a human only serves to strengthen the Martian's conviction as his narrative tails off: 'I know what it is to be an intelligent machine in a world of madness'.[23] Within a brief compass Wyndham raises questions about the relation of humans to machines and how we react to the alien, issues which were to be picked up by the novel.[24]

Stowaway to Mars, first published in 1936 under the title *Planet Plane*, was also serialized in *The Passing Show* with the title it has since retained.[25] Here it was billed as 'an epic serial of the last great exploration of all', but Wyndham carefully embeds the action in the political and technological activities of the 1930s, particularly experiments in developing rockets.[26] The narrative opens with a mysterious shooting in the hangar where the spaceship is being prepared. Clearly an attempt at sabotage, the opening suggests a national rivalry between Britain and competitors like Russia and the USA over who will manage the first flight into space. If Britain succeeds, she will achieve glory, although the craft's name, *Gloria Mundi*, part-echoes the catchphrase on the transience of worldly power – *Sic Transit Gloria Mundi* – used on the coronation of Popes. Throughout the novel Wyndham is alert to the importance of film in recording events, and the spaceship is visualized as a spectacle: 'She towered on the level plain like a monstrous shell designed for the artillery of giants' (32). The image explicitly suggests combat, as if the spaceship is an enormous weapon rather than a vessel, and the Mars expedition is set clearly within the colonial rivalries of the 1930s.

Another irony in the novel is the indication in the title of the one unplanned crew member. Joan is the daughter of the scientist who has been excluded from the expedition and who is determined to use her own training to help its completion.[27] Here we meet one of the most striking general characteristics of the novel. Wyndham's resistance to inter-planetary adventure can be seen in the way he describes the space voyage itself. Although her presence raises sexual tensions among the crew, Wyndham stresses that Joan's role is not that of the glamorous and helpless film star, but 'the part she had cast herself for was that of a young man and an equal' (80). This statement is one of many points where Wyndham invites his reader to consider how the narrative is engaging with the issues it raises and how far it is avoiding the clichés of rapid action that are common in pulp fiction. Take the case of the voyage itself. Since it is uneventful, the crew engage in a serial dialogue not only about space and the absence of gravity, but also about how such voyages have been represented in fiction. Here Wells's *Time Machine* features and also John Jacob Astor's *A Journey in Other Worlds* (1894), which is quoted to demonstrate the ambition for national glory. The role of the pilot Dale Curtance, a 'speed ace', is offset throughout by that of the scientist Froud, an author delegate whose role is to question statements and bring out their implications. Joan participates in their discussions by describing an apparently sentient machine she and her father have encountered on Earth, at which point the debate shifts to consider the meaning of 'robot', with due reference to Karel Capek, and more generally the whole relation of humanity to machines. At the beginning of Chapter 13, just before the arrival on Mars, the narrator declares: 'this is not the place to lecture upon the details of the inter-planetary journey' (98), at which point Wyndham ignores the details of the space flight, turning instead to broader issues like the relation of humanity to machines.

The extensive discussions in the first half of the novel build up a cumulative context for the arrival of the *Gloria Mundi* on Mars. Here the landscape is first described as 'desert', then as possessing vegetation. The famous canals which have been debated earlier are now confirmed as actual. More important, however, is what signs of life are there? Joan's earlier account of a sentient machine – boxlike, metallic and moving on hinged supports – has prepared us for the appearance of these creatures. Some seize her as a captive; others besiege the spaceship, but it is the former which carries the narrative forward to new discoveries. Joan serves as witness to the urban civilization of Mars which is presented cinematically in scenes reminiscent of *Metropolis,* where the height of buildings is stressed, their artificial lighting and sheer activity as the machines scurry in and out of arches. We are told:

> Her first impression was of a city of light within the city of darkness [...] She entered a vast circular hall filled with light from sources which she could not detect. The high roof was slightly domed and must, she thought, have been fully three hundred feet above her at its centre. (131–132)

As an emblem of Martian culture, the city conveys scale and geometry which dwarf the human observer. It is a purposeful utilitarian construct whose purposes are hidden by unseen passages but whose sheer order suggests a technological utopia.

The city changes significance yet again when Joan meets a man with 'reddish' skin, slightly large features, but with no characteristics that are alien or threatening. On the contrary, this figure named Vaygan gives Joan, and therefore the reader, access to the Martians' story, which he explains after giving her access to his language through telepathic projection. As perceived at the end of the nineteenth century and glimpsed through *The War of the Worlds* (1898), theirs is an old culture, technologically sophisticated but in decline. The city visited by Joan is called Hanno (after the Carthaginian explorer?), one of only seven surviving, and the culture is doomed. Wyndham's one concession to inter-planetary romance comes when Joan and Vaygan experience a moment of desire, but the coda of the novel directs its main ironies against the Earthlings' appetite for territorial expansion.

Soon after landing on Mars, Dale unfurls a Union Jack and nails it to the ground, claiming 'this land' for Britain in the name of Queen Elizabeth the Second. The novel's action takes place in the year 1981 and Wyndham shrewdly and accurately guesses the then current monarch. However, soon after this event a second rocket lands – this time from Russia – whose leader ridicules British imperialism as being outdated by the rival technologies of his own country and that of the USA. Once again, Wyndham withholds the details of the British spaceship's return. Its crew are feted as celebrities, but has that been at the cost of them disabling the Russian vessel, and what of the larger ironies represented by the Martians as a possible future for the culture of the Earth?

As if in recognition of the abrupt ending of *Stowaway to Mars*, in 1938 Wyndham published a sequel called 'Sleepers of Mars', which picks up events where the novel left them.[28] The preamble to this novella of nine chapters strengthens the grand narrative frame of the novel with its sombre generalization that 'all the planets are dying' and that Mars represents the future of Earth.[29] The focus now falls on Martian industry, its box-shaped 'workers' carrying legs, antennae and front lens, and erecting the Russian spaceship ready for take-off. However, the launch fails and the Russians are taken to another city while their spaceship is repaired. Here they learn the history of Mars – a tale of 'impotence and futility' – and discover that the Martians have been put into suspended animation in a huge underground vault, the eponymous 'sleepers'.[30] They break open one glass container, killing its inmate in the process, then successfully revive a second, who explains that the vault was a measure to deal with overpopulation. A clear tribute to Wells's *When the Sleeper Wakes*, this episode has the unexpected result of triggering a general awakening in the vault, as the sleepers rise in revolt against those who initiated the measure. The narrative ends once again with questions. Will the Russian spaceship return to Earth? Will the Russian crew member left behind commit suicide as he holds a Martian device to his head? More broadly, the reader is left wondering about the fate of humanity from this tale of technological failure and human division.

Wyndham's references to the fiction of Mars in *Castaway* is only one example of his recurrent strategy of making the evolution of science fiction part of his subject. In 'Child of Power' (1939), allusions also build up a context for the story, which concerns a young boy with a preternatural sensitivity to electricity. Ted Filler can somehow overhear telephone conversations and 'hear' electrical signals, even some from outer space. His doctor, who narrates his story, becomes fired with the thought that Ted might bring about a whole new understanding of electricity, and most of the story dramatizes the interaction between the doctor's excitement and Ted's father's desire to place his son in the music hall. The story is introduced through comparisons with other tales of child prodigies – J. D. Beresford's

The Hampdenshire Wonder (1911, US title *The Wonder*), which was to serve as a source for *The Midwich Cuckoos*, and Olaf Stapledon's *Odd John* (1935) – but Wyndham's narrative cuts off abruptly when lightning suddenly neutralizes Ted's faculty. The latter would have had clear military applications, but the subject is cut off before these can emerge.

Wyndham's fiction of the 1930s repeatedly diverts its subjects from violent adventure to speculations about perception. 'Exiles on Asperus' (1933), for example, opens with the voyage of the spaceship *Argenta* (named after a British naval prison ship) carrying Martian prisoners. Hit by an asteroid, it is forced to land on the planetoid Asperus, at which point the Martians revolt, seize the *Argenta* and leave the crew stranded on the new planet. The twists and turns in this drama take second place to the introduction of a third alien species of winged creatures on Asperus. The 'Batrachs' ('frogs' in Greek), as they are called, are introduced as 'grotesque, shrouded figures', but then progressively humanized into 'bat-men', or winged bipeds capable of rational behaviour.[31] Our heroes discover that the survivors and descendants from an earlier spaceship are being held in caves by the Batrachs, at which point the stage seems set for a narrative of liberation, until the prisoners display a pathological fear of the 'Outside'. In one case we witness a small boy crawling towards the sunlight beyond his cave, but when he reaches the exit he is driven back by a loud gong and sudden stench. A doctor immediately comments that this was a 'pure Behaviourist method' and the Batrachs prove to be truly efficient in conditioning their prisoners' responses.[32] The original periodical publication in *Wonder Stories Quarterly* carried a graphic illustration of the Batrachs, showing them as monstrous threatening creatures, whereas Wyndham plays down their appearance, showing them as alternative forms of humanity. In their meeting with the astronauts, they do not pose a physical threat but rather challenge the latter's assumptions about freedom. In effect they behave like a relocated version of the administrators of the conditioning centre in Huxley's *Brave New World* (1932), where negative responses are triggered in small children by loud sirens and electric shocks, Wyndham's probable source. What is initially set up as a species struggle with the Batrachs dissipates as soon as the two groups engage in dialogue, and the perfunctory ending pays no attention to how the astronauts will return to Earth.

In 'Exiles on Asperus', the physical conflict between humans and aliens yields priority to a dialogue on human behaviour. In 'The Lost Machine' (1932), Wyndham again reverses the notion of the alien. A header to the original publication drew a contrast between the familiar issue of how machines affect humans and the subject being presented, asking 'who has ever stopped to consider the possible reactions – or thoughts – of the advanced machine of the future? The introduction shows a machine in a scientist's laboratory dissolving and disappearing, but not before it leaves a pile of typed sheets behind – its narration. Wyndham follows a series of inversions here, primarily the reversal of the contrast between human and machine. The latter supplies the sentience of humans and even articulates an account of the comic inadequacies of their reactions to the machine, just referred to as a 'long box thing'.[33] In his introduction to the 1973 collection, Leslie Flood notes that this was 'probably the prototype of the sentient robot', but Wyndham's narrator doesn't have a quasi-human appearance.[34] While animated locomotives had appeared as early as 1895 in Kipling's '007', robot stories as such began later with Eando Binder's 'I, Robot' (1939) and more famously with Isaac Asimov's 'Robbie' (1940), which introduced a whole series.

'The Lost Machine' glances briefly at technophobia, which was to become a major theme in Asimov, when the narrator notes with astonishment 'men afraid of a machine'.[35] But Wyndham is particularly concerned to open up a broader distanced perspective on humanity, as when the following comparison is drawn: 'Men may have more powers of originality than we, and they do possess a greater degree of adaptability than any other form of life, but their limitations are, nevertheless, severe'.[36] The thoughtful reflective prose is typical of the whole narration, the keynote of which is watchful analysis, certainly not hostility. After being misunderstood and even shot at, the narrator concludes of Earth that 'this whole world is too primitive' and of 'himself' 'I am a freak [...] a curiosity outside comprehension' (5). In fact Wyndham humorously juxtaposes humans and animals in scenes using a farm and then a circus. The inset narrative concludes with a challenge to the reader as to whether we are more broad-minded than the humans within the story.

In all these stories the realist context to the action is repeatedly altered, nudging the reader towards considering different possibilities. 'The Man from Beyond' (1934), for example, ironically reverses the scenario of 'Exiles on Asperus' by setting its action on Venus and opening with a biology teacher explaining the species of different creatures in the local zoo. As he moves along the cages, he pauses at the most 'puzzling' case – a mysterious, apparently 'advanced' biped quickly recognizable as a human. Here Wyndham reverses the blatant racism of the human zoos in operation until the early twentieth century. Now the supposedly advanced human is the exhibit. This frame introduces the latter's own story of space exploration as a form of commercial imperialism. He explicitly directs his account towards the Venusians as a warning of things to come. A company clearly based on the 1930s giant, ICI, has developed a spaceship called the *Nuntia* (the 'coming thing') to check out the mineral wealth of Venus. The narrator is caught up in the enterprise by working for the rival company but planning to sabotage the *Nuntia*. Once he makes contact with the Venusians, the latter completely block any hopes for his rescue by showing him images of Earth apparently destroyed and barren of life. The story concludes with the astronaut's suicide: 'Then, deliberately, with a step that did not falter, he walked over the cliff edge'.[37] So much for the fate of the last man. The conclusion is one of Wyndham's bleakest in holding out no hope for humanity.

By the 1940s Wyndham was identifying a new conservatism and standardization in American culture which was heightening already existing tendencies in their SF: 'It is safer policy to confine prophecy as much as possible to the field of mechanical gadgets and leave the people as they are'. As a result, Wyndham concludes: 'it is much less trouble keep to a path which leads to a happy-ever-after in a gadgeteer's heaven'.[38]

Clear signs of the war to come can be seen in the stories he contributed to the short-lived London-based periodical *Fantasy: A Magazine of Thrilling Science Fiction*, which had three issues from 1938 to 1939.[39] Within a general context of warfare in this journal, Wyndham's 'Beyond the Screen', later re-titled 'Judson's

Annihilator', evokes a situation of imminent conflict within which the inventor Judson is demonstrating a new weapon which makes everything targeted disappear. When reprinted in *Amazing Stories* it carried the following editorial header: 'Thousands of warplanes roared toward England and the nation paid no heed. Abruptly there were no planes, and baffled warlords gazed at empty skies'.[40] This actually over-simplifies the story, which is essentially a study of the unexpected. After the successful trials of the annihilator, Nazi and Italian invasion forces are described, and we expect these to be destroyed and British freedom preserved. However, the perspective character Martin accidentally falls victim to the device, but stays alive. So not only does the annihilator not kill, it transports subjects to a strange alternative world located elsewhere in time. Martin is taken captive by German airmen who have suffered his fate, one of which describes his experiences of his flight being transformed. Set up initially as an enemy, he shares Martin's translocation. The story thus uses disruptions of our everyday reality to distance us from the imminent war and a moral is proposed by Judson's sister when she states: 'hasn't civilization after civilization climbed up and then fallen down this sink of war?'.[41]

Warfare similarly informs 'The Trojan Beam' (March 1939), which starts in the middle of a tank battle, not immediately identified as being waged by the Japanese in China. Once again we have a new weapon being used – a magnetic beam so strong that it could even move a tank. This is first shown when the opening Japanese offensive collapses as soldiers lose control of their tanks which burn out or run into a nearby river. Wyndham uses an English double agent to give us glimpses of both sides in the conflict. George White is actually feeding information from the Chinese to the Japanese, particularly details of the former's secret weapon. The story's title implies an analogy with the Trojan Horse in that the secret weapon is covertly passed to the Japanese not as a gift but as an ostensible security leak. In reality the Chinese fill their positions with canisters containing explosives and chemical weapons which, when drawn magnetically to the Japanese, detonate causing multiple casualties. The final crucial collapse of the Japanese is brought about when the magnetic beam is trained on a meteor shower, causing not just military collapse but also widespread destruction. Throughout his early fiction Wyndham repeatedly times his narratives at dates in the future, sometimes – as we saw in 'Worlds to Barter' – in order to speculate on possible directions of evolution. Alternatively, time might serve as a distancing device. 'The Trojan Beam' embeds us immediately within the details of a war between China and Japan (current at time of publication), but then sets its action in 1965 to push the reader back from the immediate drama to consider the nature of war. This process is helped by the protagonist being an English spy, supposedly helping the Chinese but more broadly serving as commentator on the development of hostilities.

In 'Derelict of Space' (1939) comparable close reference is made to the politics of the time, relayed by a detailed account of how a derelict spaceship is salvaged and brought back to Earth. The action takes place in a future where space travel has become well established in an extended analogy with sea trade. The narrator is an established astronaut, establishing his plausibility through the carefully detailed account of the salvage process – which goes wrong as the vessels prepare to land on Earth. The derelict loses its mooring and flies away from the other vessel, and at this point the focus of the story shifts away from the future to the politics of 1939. The narrator learns that the derelict has crashed on to a German village causing massive explosions. Or perhaps there was only a single detonation. And to make matters worse, one of the salvage crew is shot in London and an attempt made on the life of the captain. The British Secret Service are drawn in and explain that the Germans were secretly using the town as a base for covert explosive research. When the German authorities fail to muffle the publicity over the event, they recast the news as external aggression: 'Jewish influence, combining behind the Jewish Captain Belford, had aimed a blow at the defences of the Reich; the first blow in the covert war which World Jewry was opening against Germany'.[42] By this point it has become clear that the bulk of the story is an irrelevance to the climax. Not even the gold being carried by the derelict is important compared with the chance detonation at the German base. As the political tension mounts, the narrator and his captain are given new identities and spirited away from public scrutiny. Although we are told that the action took place 'a long time ago', Wyndham's coda brings the story into direct topical relevance to its publication date.

Wyndham's stories from the late 1930s show a growing disenchantment with scientific inventions which carry military applications. 'Judson's Annihilator' was the new title given to what was originally called more abstractly 'Beyond the Screen', and the change foregrounds the inventor's responsibility. The story culminates in an image of widespread destruction, and in the 'Meet the Authors' column for the issue of *Amazing Stories* where the story appeared, Wyndham explained that it was inspired by a statement from H. G. Wells that 'the military caste always regards the scientist as a kind of gifted inferior'. Mulling over the implications, Wyndham reflected that there was no need to draw on the cliché of the mad scientist since the scientist was a promoter of weaponry. Not only that, he continues, 'who is one of the chief drawers of royalties when the soldiers are blown up? The scientist. Who is it who should be the priest of progress, but is content to behave with the irresponsibility of a half-wit?'[43] In the story, Judson doesn't come across as a half-wit so much as a clever entertainer throwing stones to a military observer, which in no way foreshadows the massive spectacle of destruction which will follow from his invention.

In 1939 Britain declared war and Wyndham lived through the London Blitz which followed, serving as a censor for the Ministry of Information until in 1943 he began his military service in the Royal Corps of Signals.[44] There followed a long hiatus in his writing until 1946 when he began to publish fiction again and was to write his major works.

2

Triffids and Other Invasions

THE DAY OF THE TRIFFIDS

The Day of the Triffids (1951), with its twin premises of widespread blinding from a passing comet and an invasion of predatory plants, marked Wyndham's major entry into the postwar fiction market. Although he recalled that he received some hostile reviews ('Pooter' 1968), it has remained his most popular and recently his most-analysed novel. It was originally planned as part of a future-history sequence with a climax of bacterial and chemical warfare, but this was abandoned.[1]

The novel opens by announcing, but understating, the apocalyptic subject of the 'end of the world', which the narrator William Masen somehow contrived to miss. The apparent contradiction in the first chapter title – 'The End Begins' – dislocates the reader just as Masen is disoriented on the morning when he begins his account, but, as several critics have noted, the title echoes Churchill's declaration after the battle of Alamein of the 'end of the beginning'. Temporarily blinded after an operation, he is totally dependent on sounds for his bearings in time. His description assembles absences, silences all suggesting the lack of the normal morning activities he would expect in his hospital. Masen thus establishes himself as a narrator deprived of even the most basic sense data about his own situation. He is, in short, defined by his attempts to discover and explain what is happening around him.

As soon as his memory begins to function, he recalls all the news reports from the previous evening of the Earth passing through a 'cloud of meteor debris', which flashes constantly with a green light, a colour probably suggested to Wyndham by H. G. Wells's 1906 novel *In the Days of the Comet*, where a comet spreading green light in the skies induces a euphoric transformation in humanity.[2] For Wyndham's narrator, spectacle morphs into assault, however, when he realizes that everyone who witnessed the flashing lights has been blinded. In a pointedly ironic reversal, Masen regains his vision just at the moment when apparently everyone else has lost theirs. Late in the novel a character questions the reality of the comet, speculating that it might have been some kind of 'satellite weapon'. Apart from Wells, whose story 'The Country of the Blind' is quoted at one point, Wyndham also quotes the catchphrase 'it can't happen here' to sum up a collective national complacency which *The Day of the Triffids* undermines. This phrase figured as title to Sinclair Lewis's 1935 novel about the rise of a dictator within the USA. Although the latter's context was clearly different, Lewis's warning performed a similar role to Wyndham's in startling the reader into questioning our sense of possibility.

The triffids are introduced through the context of Cold War superpower rivalries, specifically through satellites, although at the time of publication Sputnik was still four years off. Wyndham carefully orders his explanations to foreground the weaponization of satellites which could drop missiles of any form once these were in orbit. From missiles we transition to a company promising a new cheap means of providing edible oil. The origins of this company are never specified; its agent is associated with South America. Apparently the Soviet Union develops the triffids because reports emerge of a triffid station in the Far East. Then the Soviet agent disappears and there are signs that the company agent's plane blows up, expelling a huge 'cloud of seeds' (27). Masen stresses that his whole account is 'conjecture', but its uncertainties play directly to a reader's anxieties in the early 1950s, of covert experiments with biological weapons and crops. The Soviet geneticist Trofim Lysenko is named here, notorious for his experiments with species modification. Wyndham strategically allows this discussion to play to the reader's paranoid suspicions that Britain (and the rest of the world) is under attack before he fills in more details about the triffids.

Before we go further, however, it is important to recognize the subtle shifts in the narrative voice which take place throughout the novel. As we saw in the opening, Masen is grappling with incongruous silences in his hospital. He does this by examining himself, especially focusing on the tensions between his fears and his efforts to understand what is happening to him. In so doing he establishes his own credibility by denying himself any privileged awareness of events. Through him the reader is thus embedded in the immediate physical circumstances of a city bizarrely reduced to silence by the pandemic blindness. As he struggles to explain his situation, Masen uses one of the many allusions to Wells when he declares: 'Looking back at the shape of things then, the amount we did not know and did not care to know about our daily lives is not only astonishing, but somehow a bit shocking' (9). For Wells the 'shape of things to come' represented our imminent future, whereas Wyndham throughout the novel sets up a serial contrast between how our sense of reality has been based on habits which cataclysmic events have undermined. Contrasts between past and present run throughout the novel, but these become further nuanced by Masen's constant care to show how things are represented through the media, and his self-scrutiny to avoid making his account too definite. Thus the information about the origin of the triffids remains speculative.[3]

Throughout the novel Masen's care over shaping his account constitutes an important part of his narrative, frequently giving it a meta-dimension. For example, early in the novel he sees a young woman being beaten by a blind man who wants to use her as a guide. After rescuing her, he sizes up her appearance as conforming to a 'film-director's idea of the heroine' (52). Josella at this point is also aware of styles of behaviour, admitting to melodramatic terror when she discovers the pandemic blindness in London. She performs a role shared by most of Masen's contacts, namely to engage in a dialogue on how to react to the extraordinary events taking place. How to react to events thus becomes the novel's repeated question, and even the chapter titles like 'Shadows Before', 'Frustration' and 'Dead End' signal provisional glosses on the episodes as they take place. Late in the novel Masen records that he started keeping a journal to help him keep track of material necessities. From that point on he becomes a reader and interpreter of his own record.

Wyndham could have taken the idea for *Triffids* stories dealing with modified plants from between the wars from Edmond Hamilton's 'The Plant Revolt' (1930), where plants stop growing roots and become ambulatory with the help of tendrils.[4] Or he might have known Laurence Manning's 1935 story 'Seeds from Space', where again 'trees' become capable of 'walking' on three roots.[5] The cover image for *Wonder Stories*, where the story appeared, showed a clear boll with roots and arm-like branches, which partly anticipates the image of a triffid devised for the novel in the 1950s. The main source for Wyndham's novel, however, can be found in his own 1933 story called 'The Puff-Ball Menace' (also published under the title 'Spheres of Hell'). This first appeared in *Wonder Stories* with a brief preamble on the 'scientific ingenuity for warfare' shown by Japan towards China. The story opens in the eastern state of Ghangistan, a clear echo of Genghis Khan, the leader of the Mongol Empire, which is on the verge of warfare with Britain. A 'man of learning' in the former country designs organisms which are distributed to the West, where each is described as a 'ball of blotchy, virulent yellow'.[6] This updated yellow peril swells until it explodes, emitting poisonous spores which 'prey' on their English victims. The invasion is met with the army deploying flame throwers, but the attack actually fails because the fungus providentially metamorphoses into a conventional, non-aggressive species.[7] While working on *Triffids*, Wyndham reviewed Ward Moore's *Greener Than You Think* (1947), which describes the invention of a 'metamorphizer' capable of changing the structure of plants. When the salesman narrator sprays a Los Angeles lawn with this liquid (conceived as an 'inoculation') the Bermuda grass grows uncontrollably in California and then around the world.[8]

Apart from literary sources, in interview Wyndham explained that one immediate source for the triffids lay in the English countryside: 'one night when I was walking along a dark lane in the country and the hedges were only just distinguishable against the sky and the higher things sticking up from the hedges became rather menacing and one felt that they might come over and strike down'.[9] Wyndham's partner Grace Wilson further added the complications of sentience and mobility, 'how dangerous it would be if they could think and move'.[10]

There is no hint of reprieve in *The Day of the Triffids*. Roger Luckhurst has argued that the 'triffids are merely the occasion for what propels the plot: an episodic encounter with different kinds of community in the wake of the disaster'.[11] However, while it is obviously true that the coming of the triffids gives the narrative its basic impetus, the creatures are never forgotten. As we have already seen, they are contextualized within the Soviet Union's secret biological experiments and secondly within contemporary agriculture. The narrator's back story of himself in the second chapter includes his memories of his father scrutinizing a half-grown triffid, and his own experience of falling unconscious after being lashed by a mature triffid. There is even an inset on the term 'triffid' as a 'catchy little name originating in some newspaper office' (31). They are thus established as familiar creatures, but also as a threat, not least from the striking accuracy of their lashes, which are always directed at the head or an exposed limb, but also from their carnivorous attraction to rotting flesh. A friend of Masen's is convinced that triffids can 'talk' by beating their 'little sticks' against their bodies, and their seed-time is described as a 'bombardment' of spores (35). The startling discovery that they can walk – on three legs like Wells's Martians in *The War of the Worlds* – blurs the conventional distinction between flora and fauna, establishing them as a mysterious hybrid species, puzzling Masen and his associates right to the end of the novel.[12] A clear development in the plot is the regression of cities, particularly London, towards a pre-industrial state which takes place in tandem with a steady increase in the numbers of triffids. They are referred to variously as plants, animals and even barbaric humans. Wells reverses the direction of empire in the invasion of the Martians. Wyndham follows the same trajectory in his triffids, which are referred to as 'brutes', and which themselves wield 'lashes', a prime symbol of colonial authority.[13] The abridged serialization which appeared in *Collier's* makes this issue explicit in its title – 'Revolt of the Triffids' – and in the suggestion that the creatures have originated in colonies on Venus.[14]

Although they recede into the background of some episodes, they remain an implicit presence and a focus for speculation about their species.[15] The girl Susan identifies their sensitivity to sounds, which in turn raises questions about their responses. Late in the novel Masen posits a collective intelligence to their behaviour, much more evident in large groups. Masen's partner Josella insists that 'they're so *different'*, adding that they may possess a 'gene of social organization' like bees, but without any conclusion (209). Physically and intellectually they pose a multiple threat – to human survival and to characters' assumptions of their generic superiority. This is reflected in the gradual contraction of safe space throughout the novel, as if the triffids are gradually displacing the humans.

Clearly the triffids pose a direct threat throughout the novel, and Masen encounters a whole series of groups who are in their different ways trying to organize means of coping with the crisis. The first such group in London consists of a line of blind men being led by a sighted leader calling out orders to them. They resemble a travesty military line-up being used to justify any opportunities for looting. Initially more positive is the gathering Masen and Josella join at the University of London's Senate House, a setting used by George Orwell as a model for the Ministry of Truth in *Nineteen Eighty-Four*, which Wyndham read soon after publication while working on his own novel.[16] The military dimension to the group is embodied by its leader, referred to simply as 'the colonel', but other figures more importantly add to or challenge Masen's understanding of the evolving situation. Loosely based on one of Wyndham's teachers, Michael Beadley takes his bearings in the crisis not from the triffids but from the bombing of Nagasaki, implying a measure of human responsibility for events. Beadley's pragmatic commentary is offset by an address by a sociologist called Vorless (whose name suggests the German '*Vorleser'*, ie 'reader'). He insists that '*the race is worth preserving'* (99–100, his emphasis), which instrumentalizes the surviving women as child-bearing vessels. So soon after the war, it would be difficult to miss the echoes here of the Nazis' racial programme and this sets one of the keynotes for most of the groups Masen encounters. These usually attempt to deal with the crisis by returning to organizations from the past.[17]

Any kind of restoration pulls against the novel's geographical progression as Masen and his companions move farther and farther from London, the symbolic centre of national and imperial order. Further echoes of the war emerge in Chapter 9 ('Evacuation'), where Masen bids farewell to Westminster, reflecting on the symbolism of the Thames which 'would flow until the day [...] Westminster became once more an island in a marsh' (128). In tandem with this future evolutionary reversion, Masen also registers what he later describes in Darwinian terms as the loss of the 'herd' of the group, necessary for the survival of the species.

This loss emerges through a recurring irony in the evacuation process. As Masen seeks new refuges, he realizes that he faces serious danger not only from the triffids but also from other survivors, several times being shot at. Provisional safety seems to be offered in Tynsham Manor near Devizes, which however proves to be a puritanical Christian community so repressive that Masen has to move on. His main companion at this point is William Coker, who enters the novel leading a gang which raids London University but then experiences a change of heart and joins Masen in the search for a viable refuge. Wyndham has been criticized (eg by Link 2015) for presenting middle-class characters, although this underestimates Masen's self-scrutiny throughout. Coker further challenges this class stereotyping because he explains himself to Masen as a 'hybrid', a character of working-class origins who is able to adjust his behaviour to the expectations of others. More than that, he overtly challenges the assumptions of figures like the director of Tynsham, and when a girl claims ignorance of machines, she is attacked by Coker for yielding to 'myth and affectation' rendered offensive by the current emergency (149). It's possible that Wyndham chose Coker's name to echo East Coker in T. S. Eliot's *Four Quartets*, and he does demonstrate a familiarity with poetry, but his main function remains that of challenging Masen's assumptions about survival.

The most positive refuge Masen finds seems to be Shirning Farm in Sussex, which he organizes with Josella after their reunion as a small self-contained community. However, true to the austere logic of the novel, nowhere is truly safe. The triffids mass more threateningly round the farm boundary and they are visited by Torrence, a commander in the local militia which has been set up there and in other centres around the country, and who offers Masen a supervisor's role in what would become a 'feudal seigneury'. Using the Darwinian imperative 'this is a matter of survival' (226) as a catch-all justification, he attempts to impose a regulation of how many sighted people should cohabit with the blind, and insists that Masen has no choice but to accede to his demands. And so once again evacuation becomes essential, this time to the Isle of Wight, which, as Nicholas Ruddick has shown, represents the proxy substitute for Britain.[18] And there the novel concludes, except for a brief coda which segues from Masen's narrative to another's 'excellent history of the colony' (233) and the pious hope that survivors will struggle to wipe out the triffids.[19]

In *The Death of Grass*, the 1956 novel by Wyndham's friend John Christopher (the pen name of Sam Youd), the narrative also traces the breakdown of order in Britain as a virus arrives from Asia which destroys grass and grain crops. The government falls and violence breaks out all over the country because, as the protagonist explains to his son, 'We have to fight to live'.[20] Although the narrative resembles Wyndham's in dramatizing a natural disaster which disrupts society, two aspects contrast with *The Day of the Triffids*. The core family unit of the protagonist survives throughout, giving a relative security missing in Wyndham, and the novel begins and ends in Westmoreland which persists as a refuge, however precarious. Exactly how and where characters may survive in Wyndham's novel, however, remains an open issue. Both novels bring into question anthropocentric presumptions, raising issues of plant sentience.[21]

PLAN FOR CHAOS

While working on *Triffids*, Wyndham was also composing a narrative about a Nazi revival, and David Ketterer has argued that both novels are linked through the issue of genetic experimentation.[22] *Plan for Chaos* (originally to be called *Fury of Creation* and first published in 2009), dramatizes the resurgence of a secret Nazi organization, based possibly in South America, which is planning world conquest through a 'New Germany' equipped with the technical means of multiple cloning and the new technology of satellite weapons.[23] The story is narrated by Johnny Farthing, a photographer of Swedish and British blood (originally American), who discovers that a recent number of deaths have involved women who closely resembled each other. Following the hard-boiled formula and style, the first half of the novel traces his investigation of this mystery in a city which is unnamed, but which is possibly New York. Gradually evidence begins to emerge of a conspiracy which has been registered by the security agencies, and in his search for 'Headquarters', Johnny is taken on a flight to another unnamed country where he discovers the working of the organization and finally meets its matriarch, known simply as 'The Mother', who appears as if through a cinema 'dissolve', emerges 'from a page that was almost fiction', and who briefly resembles Johnny's own mother.[24] She explains at length the ideology underpinning their plans, stressing that Germany to them represents 'a faith, an ideal' which they are trying to realize through a new concept of warfare through genetic multiplication and the use of new space vehicles resembling flying saucers. Both cloning and atomic weapons are linked as using kinds of fission. A gathering of the members recapitulates Nazi rallies with Hitler's role being replaced by that of Mother, but the event is disrupted by a scientist – loosely based on the Nazi geneticist Josef Mengele – who is shot, then replaced by another would-be leader, and the gathering breaks down into chaos.

Although *Plan for Chaos* was initially billed as a 'prequel to *The Day of the Triffids*', there are major differences between the two works, although they are linked thematically through genetic experimentation and flying saucers. *Triffids* constantly embeds its mystery in the detailed circumstances of everyday life in Britain, whereas the other work never even names its settings. It is also an essentially backward-looking narrative attempting to present a racial ideology of the 1930s, articulated through statements like the one from a member of the association who declares that 'to be of a race is not a thing one can cease' (135). In *Plan for Chaos* the process of multiple cloning could have been related to Mengele's concentration camp experiments, but once again this is left implicit. The process is never actually explained and may well owe more to the Bokanovsky Process in *Brave New World*. Ira Levin's 1976 novel *The Boys from Brazil*, in contrast with Wyndham, keeps its theme of Nazi resurgence tied to the historical figure of Mengele, who has taken genetic material from Hitler to use in his plan to create a new Reich, based in South America but using the ODESSA network. When Yakov Liebermann, the Nazi-hunter narrator, tracks down the young clones (who, ironically, slightly resemble the children in *The Midwich Cuckoos*), they raise sinister questions about their future, whereas it remains unclear how Wyndham's figures will penetrate society. We do not learn much more than the fact that they are planning an 'Action Day' when they will cause the chaos of the title, and the narrative concludes with discussions of how disaster stories are given gendered colouring. Wyndham later reflected that the whole subject had been 'mistimed'.[25]

THE KRAKEN WAKES

The Kraken Wakes (1953) narrates another invasive process, but now shifts our concern to the ocean depths where 'fireballs' fall, apparently from outer space. We are introduced to the narrator, a radio journalist called Mike Watson (who chooses the narrative's title), speculating with his wife Phyllis about how to compose a narrative of the ocean. They choose an epigraph from Tennyson's poem 'The Kraken'. Despite the foregrounding of the ocean, the origins of the novel's mystery emerge from outer space. During a cruise near the Azores, Watson and his wife see strange objects fly through the sky and plunge into the ocean. At this point we should pause over the first line of the narrative proper. Watson declares: 'I'm a reliable witness' and the novel repeatedly returns to how mysteries are reported and explained. In one sense the news media make up the collective protagonist, and Watson's role – along with that of Phyllis who engages in strenuous dialogues with him at every point – is to comment on events and the different ways they are interpreted.[26] Unlike the triffids which are visualized from the very beginning of their novel, the mysterious apparitions seen in the sky have no shape, only colour, being described as 'pink fuzz, with a deep red centre' (18). They are later referred to as 'fireballs' and their proxy creations as 'sea-tanks', but at no point do we ever see them. For most of the novel they remain enigmas hidden in the deepest parts of the oceans and the reader is constantly posed with the problem of how to refer to them.

During his composition of the novel, Wyndham explained to the editor of Ballantine Books that he wanted to avoid the usual anthropomorphic pattern of interplanetary invasion. Instead 'the idea here was to get a menace that was alien [...] so much so that nobody is even quite certain whether there is an interplanetary war going on, or not'. Since so little is understood about the invading creatures, the novel purports to be a story of a mystery rather than that of an interplanetary war'.[27]

Tennyson's Kraken is an individual local monster, whereas the creatures in the novel pose a more sinister threat in being apparently dispersed around the world. Wyndham sets his story within the historical context of the nuclear tests in the Pacific and the superpower confrontations of the Cold War. Thus after each local crisis there is a flurry of news reports with predictable responses from the Soviets – when they comment at all. Shortly after the appearance of the fuzz-balls the Admiralty deploys one of its latest instruments – a 'telebath' – to explore the depths of the ocean. At first it just registers a 'large uncertain oval shape', i.e. no discernible creature, but then the line goes dead. It emerges that somehow the electric cables have become fused together. This latest event, together with the mysterious sinking of different vessels, convinces the British authorities that an 'intelligence' is at work, but what kind of intelligence and with what purpose remains unknown. The stakes rise as more and more sinkings happen until the decision is taken to drop nuclear bombs on the 'creatures', triggering a fresh wave of paranoia when two of the devices fail to detonate.

Essentially then *The Kraken Wakes* is a mystery narrative. Different events are reported in dry matter-of-fact tones and then the different media all present their interpretations. Characters' roles reflect their different perspectives on events, one arguing that everything is being guided by a rational intelligence, another arguing that Moscow is using its midget submarines to direct a conspiracy. At one point Phyllis explains that they are all 'trying to fit a lot of bits and pieces into a puzzle' (63), which could stand as a comment on the novel's method as a whole. Wyndham releases data in a montage of brief fragments.[28] A Japanese cruiser liner sinks with brief reports of the women and children screaming in panic. An American task force in the Caribbean is covered by verbal commentary dissolving into panic when the leading destroyer and frigate are blown up. When the surviving vessels try to make a getaway, the reporter's voice simply breaks off as he exclaims 'The whole sea's –' (97). The USA tries to forestall a second Pearl Harbor and the British prime minister tries to rally Parliament in supporting the 'Battle of the Deeps' with another implicit parallel to the Second World War. And all this time the sea creatures remain a mystery. We learn that they are predatory in dispatching 'creatures' with very long tentacles which can carry off humans, but this detail – probably a concession to Wells – sheds no further light on their purpose. They simply remain, as an admiral explains, 'artificial organic constructions' (153).[29]

The most graphic account of an attack by the invading organisms comes in Phase Two on the Caribbean island of Escondida (i.e. 'hidden'). The situation is contextualized historically as well as geographically through references to the Spanish and British empires. Then, during the night observers get their first glimpse of the so-called 'sea-tanks', each one resembling 'an elongated egg which has been halved down its length and set flat side to the ground' (138). On one level it seems as if the competition for empire is being replayed by these organisms, which swell up like enormous bladders, finally bursting open emitting white cilia. Wyndham plays on the reader's startled curiosity to suggest parts of an organism never seen or understood in its entirety. He also plays on disproportion in that cilia are normally tiny, hair-like attachments, but here they function as organs of attack 'like long white whiplashes' (140) which attach themselves to humans and attempt to draw them back into a central consuming organism. In short, like a biological parable of empire, they attempt to consume the inhabitants of the area under attack. They are based in the depths of the ocean rather than on its surface as were the original imperial navies. To name them as 'xenobaths' – literally 'alien creatures of the deep' – captures the incomprehension of the human observers. In that respect the US title for the novel – *Out of the Deeps* – better captures their mystery than the title with the Kraken, since the creatures are never seen in their entirety.

Wyndham's decision to break his novel up into 'phases' suggests that a process is taking place which humanity can't yet understand. Phase 2 concludes with a series of attacks on Santander, Ireland, and other locations. Phase 3 opens with a radical change to the narrator's circumstances. Where news reports were earlier analysed to give us glimpses of an evolving worldwide situation, the focus now falls locally on the narrator and his wife in a dinghy, feeling their way forward as if they are being monitored or pursued. As the narrator attempts to cut a hole in a net blocking their way, gunshots ring out and a voice (English) warns him to stay away. Via the Cold War, the earlier sections had filtered the emerging crisis through the superpower confrontations of the 1950s. Now hostilities have broken out within Britain. It gradually emerges that the polar icecaps have been melting with the result that the sea level has risen so much that Britain has been flooded. This shift in descriptive focus has led one critic to describe the novel as the 'first work of climate fiction',[30] but while he is right that characters wilfully refuse to face the changes taking place, their causal relation to human actions remains complex and oblique.

If the invasive forces are imagined as a species, they are presented from a Darwinian perspective as engaged in a struggle for supremacy, but not as explicitly as Richard Jefferies's *After London* (1885), whose opening section is titled 'Relapse into Barbarism'.[31] Echoes of the Second World War proliferate as looting breaks out in some areas and sandbags are mounted against the 'attack' of the rising waters. Opinion remains divided about whether the bombing of the 'Bathies' has been successful, and Watson and Phyllis witness a massive surge of high water which breaks the Thames Embankment and floods the city. The novel's coda gives the last word to Phyllis, who declares: '"I think we've been here before, Mike ... And we got through last time..."' (239). The ellipses leave it open whether they will 'get through', suggesting an ongoing process whose outcome is uncertain. One version of *Kraken* concludes with a scientist reflecting on a stranded 'sea-tank' that 'this may have been due to failure to breed, or to adapt, or to risk disease, or to any of the other causes which it is popularly ascribed', which even more explicitly leaves causality open.[32]

THE CHRYSALIDS

All four of Wyndham's major works punctuate their narratives with references to the Cold War, but *The Chrysalids* (1955) is most explicit. In an article of 1962 Wyndham explained the subject of *The Chrysalids* as follows:

In 'The Chrysalids' I imagined what the world might be like long after an atomic war [...] The chief concern of the surviving communities of normal mankind then became to keep the freaks at bay, and rid themselves of any variations from what they considered to be the true human form.[33]

The novel describes how a future community in Labrador operates in the aftermath of an apocalyptic cataclysm, probably that of a nuclear war, although it is only late in the novel that there are references to the 'black glass' of a blasted landscape. This is referred to simply as the 'Tribulation', the biblical term used for the 'last days' or 'end time', as the culmination of God's purpose.[34] To the authorities then the regime is beyond fault and any criticism becomes an act of sacrilege. The novel's present is a point in the future, which has brought about a reversion to a pre-industrial past. It is likely that Wyndham took a lead here from the American George R. Stewart's 1949 novel *Earth Abides*, which describes how a California community of survivors grows after an epidemic has almost wiped out the population. Stewart explores the complex relation of humanity to local flora and charts how the group reconstitutes itself through following simpler methods of agriculture. The novel was the first to win the International Fantasy Award in 1951, an award which Wyndham helped establish. One of the working titles for *The Chrysalids* was *Much Abides*.

However, a major difference between the two works lies in their treatment of Christianity. Stewart took his title from the book of Ecclesiastes, whereas Wyndham right from the start shows his society to be a repressive theocracy reinforced by slogans like 'THE NORM IS THE WILL OF GOD' and 'KEEP PURE THE STOCK OF THE LORD'. In that respect the novel resembles Leigh Brackett's 1955 novel *The Long Tomorrow*, where survivors of a nuclear holocaust in the USA find themselves in a strict fundamentalist community whose practices the adolescent protagonists are determined to resist. For Stewart the Bible helps in reconstruction; in Wyndham it functions as the source of authoritarian statements designed to close off discussion. Religion is presented politically as a means of enforcing conformity through fear and inducing a culture of concealment. The novel alludes back to Nazi practice in the authorities' concern to maintain the 'Purity of the Race', as an Inspector puts it, and also glances at McCarthyism in the requirement to carry 'Normalcy Certificates'.

In short, the society we encounter has devoted itself to blanking out the past as a 'long oblivion' and constantly reinforcing its maintenance of timeless, religiously authorized absolutes. It is a culture where implicitly all books except the Bible and the Book of Tribulation are not just forbidden, as happens in Orwell's *Nineteen Eighty-Four*, but erased from the collective consciousness. From the very beginning this places the novel itself counter to the law, as frequently happens in dystopian fiction.

The Chrysalids is narrated by David Strorm, who is ten at the beginning, but whose commentary and witness are clearly built up retrospectively to those of an adult. David is also metaphorically related to the novel's title. As the pupa of butterflies, 'chrysalis' suggests a creature in evolution, about to change to a different form, a point lost by the US title *Re-Birth*.[35] David himself and the other children he encounters are thus placed within a context of change which pulls against the static norms of their society. Throughout the novel children's perspectives are privileged over those of the adults, implicitly revealing the routine cruelty and dogmatism of the latter. When the novel was serialized in *Argosy* magazine, it carried a header quotation from Wyndham stating: 'We are no longer interested in this or that scientific marvel [...] We want to know what it will do to us and our children – to the people of tomorrow'.[36] A number of critics have recognized the novel's constant questioning of norms and the complex interplay between social order and change.[37] Particularly useful is Rowland Wymer's argument that the transformation in the novel's title introduces a chilling prioritization of survival at all costs.[38]

This inevitable tension – more severe than a simple tension between adult and child – has its linguistic dimension. When David tries unsuccessfully to bandage his injured hand, he comments spontaneously: 'I could have managed it all right by myself if I'd had another hand' (26). The adults around him freeze and his father interrogates him over his 'unnatural' desire for an extra limb. Here we encounter a major theme running throughout the novel. Since the late 1940s, fiction and film had been emerging which articulated fears of nuclear war and of radiation generally.

A similar anxiety emerges in *The Chrysalids*, articulated in the placard 'WATCH THOU FOR THE MUTANT!' and in the fear that malformed animals and humans might be produced without the authorities knowing. David's impromptu comment plays directly to this fear, which he negotiates early in the novel when he encounters a girl with six toes on one foot. This marks a peak in the drama because David has to promise secrecy, otherwise the girl and her family will be arrested. The institutionalized fear of mutation outweighs any actual cases shown in the novel. It is only much later in the novel that David encounters any mutants, whose description is introduced by the statement 'there was nothing immediately alarming about the group' (159). One has an extra finger on one hand, another a hairless head, and another unusually long limbs. Wyndham had planned to include a man with a third eye in the middle of his forehead but decided to drop that image, perhaps because it would have brought his description too close to sensational images of extraterrestrials.[39]

Wyndham introduces a variation on 'mutant' which in effect challenges the whole category. David has the ability to communicate telepathically with his half-cousin Rosalind and, as his narrative progresses, a whole sub-group of children emerge with this ability. David describes this form of communication as an inexplicable but natural extension of their normal faculties, thereby confirming his narrative credentials as a truth-teller. For the authorities, however, telepathy constitutes the ultimate subversive mutation. It cannot be seen, thereby challenging their fetishization of the 'ideal' human image, nor can it be controlled except by killing the participants, which they almost certainly do later in the novel when two telepathic children are arrested. For the state, every deviation from the norm is a distortion, but telepathy is conveyed as an extension of communication, a kind of messaging somehow below the verbal through a projection of 'thought shapes'.

Wyndham's evocation of gifted children was in line with other SF from the 1950s, particularly by the American writer Henry Kuttner, known to Wyndham since their dealings with the magazine *Wonder Stories* in the 1930s. Kuttner's *Mutant* (1953) connects with *The Chrysalids* in being a collection of stories of children created through radiation who have a hairless head, hence the title of the Baldy series. Wyndham's David has dreams of Sealand induced by telepathy and Kuttner's Baldies too have extended memories longer than their lifespan, and the narrator of *Mutant*, who links the stories rather like David, repeatedly stresses how the telepaths create a new community, declaring in his coda: *'We are one. We are man. The long, long war is ended'.*[40] Wyndham's telepaths also create the hope for a new phase of humanity.

This is partly achieved through the descriptions of David's younger sister Petra, who possesses a telepathic faculty of exceptional range. It is she who serves as a medium for communicating with the outsiders of the novel, the Sealanders who appear to live in a world nearest to that of the reader. Although she is presented as the child of the telepaths, cared for by David as a proxy parent, Petra and Rosalind play the important role of extending David's narrative, so that the latter's accounts are often typographically indistinguishable from David's. Also Rosalind steps well beyond gender stereotypes, even killing when necessary.

David's growth is significantly strengthened by Rosalind and Petra, but we need first to consider how the novel progresses topographically. The opening scenes take place in David's home, the bastion of his father's authority, then the action opens out into the local farmland, on to the Fringes, and finally to the Badlands, an area feared and demonized because unknown. As we move outwards, David appears to be gradually experiencing a liberation from his restrictive childhood. However, his progression actually takes him into greater physical danger. He is attacked and twice loses consciousness. He refers to his new situation in the wilderness several times as a 'war'. David also encounters a series of characters who encourage him to question the dogmatic values of his society. In the Fringes he encounters a dirty ragged man who gives him a quick rejoinder to his upbringing by insisting that 'God doesn't have any last word [...] He changes and grows, like everything else that's alive' (153).

Permanent change is also a message coming from Sealand, a symbolic outside world possibly suggested by Aldous Huxley's *Ape and Essence* (1949), where a team of scientists from New

Zealand visit America after its destruction in a nuclear war. In *The Chrysalids*, a spokeswoman shifts the model of endless change onto humanity, declaring that 'the living form defies evolution at its peril; if it does not adapt it will be broken' (182). The fate of the Old People is recapitulated, but now with divine displeasure being replaced by evolutionary inevitability. Each explanation is equally absolute. Also when a Sealander helicopter appears – not described as such but recognizable to the reader – apparently to rescue David and his companions, mysterious organic 'strands' are emitted which attach to the onlookers, killing the majority.

Here we encounter one of the main ambiguities of *The Chrysalids*. Most of the action has traced out an escape narrative where David and his companions attempt to flee the repressive agents of their society. The novel has become very popular with schools because it seems to lend itself to liberal criticisms of social and religious restrictions, but that is to ignore Wyndham's ambiguities, as some critics have noted.[41]

The arrival of the Sealanders can be read as a positive step towards David's ultimate liberation and implies that he will shortly be joining an external technological culture familiar to that of the reader. Again in contrast, the Sealanders' first demonstration of their technology is a military one. Their craft arrives in the middle of a battle between the men of the Fringes and those from David's home community, dropping multiple organic 'strands' which paralyze, then kill their opponents. The 'disquisition' of the Sealander woman is yet another passage of instruction to David which claims the right to kill and to prohibit. She declares that 'there have to be vegetables forbidden to flower, seeds forbidden to germinate' (195). After all his struggles forward it is ironic that David is still being forewarned of prohibitions, this time with evolutionary necessity replacing Christian absolutism. Even the imagery of this episode is ambiguous. The girls are warned that they should remove the crosses worn on the front of their dresses. On the other hand David visualizes the Sealander as a saint-like figure: 'against the thrown-back white hood, her beautiful head looked as though it were framed by a halo' (193). Does Wyndham imply that David has not actually distanced himself from the Christian culture he was fleeing? For all the tropes of opening and revelation on the novel's final page, these questions remain.[42]

THE MIDWICH CUCKOOS

The Midwich Cuckoos (1957) returns us to contemporary middle England with the sudden impregnation of the women in a village, apparently by brood parasitic aliens. Described by Margaret Atwood as Wyndham's masterpiece and a parable on unwanted pregnancies,[43] the novel follows the same pattern as *Triffids* and *Kraken* in evoking everyday life before introducing a major disruption.[44] Midwich is the stereotypical English village, where nothing extraordinary happens; it has 'drowsed upon its good soil in Arcadian undistinction for a thousand years' (12). The novel opens with an apparently minor disruption when the narrator Richard Gayford is returning to the village after birthday celebrations in London, only to find that his road has been blocked by the police, as has every other means of access. When Gayford and his wife try to enter the village across the fields, first she collapses and then himself. Quietly other disruptions accumulate. Phone links are broken; traffic accidents are registered on the access roads; finally the army is called in, suggesting a possibility to be developed that the village is somehow under attack.

The gradual progression of events up to the revelation of the children is made possible partly by the authorities' decision to exclude the press as far as possible. This in turn reflects the security concerns of the 1950s, an unease about what 'Ivan' may be up to, as one character remarks. Although the police obviously play their part in restoring order after it has been revealed that all living creatures have been unconscious in Midwich for several hours, their activities are supplemented by those of the army, including military intelligence, whose representative invites Gayford to 'keep an eye' on the village. It is the army which discovers the circular extent of what becomes referred to as the 'Dayout' and also finds possible traces of a large vessel having landed in the village.

The village serves as a synecdoche for the nation, also containing the second major unit in the novel – the family, which comes under severe pressure when the women of Midwich discover that they have become pregnant. Given the taboos of the period, this becomes difficult even to discuss and adds extra urgency to keeping events in the village away from external scrutiny. At the time of publication, it was common practice to separate illegitimate children from their mothers and abortion was strictly forbidden, all of which helps to contextualize the novel's action and to reveal the importance of the character Angela Zellaby. As wife of the scientist Gordon Zellaby, of whom more in a moment, she is one of the leading members of Midwich, and once the pregnancies are discovered, she rallies all the affected women in a meeting where she urges mutual support and confronting the practicalities of their situation. Although this is an important moment in the village, on the whole Angela is overshadowed by her husband, who gives a serial commentary on events. It was to redress this perceived imbalance that the 2022 Sky TV remake of *The Midwich Cuckoos* changed the gender of the Zellaby figure to foreground the importance of the female participants in the action by making them more vocal and presenting the action as a drama of motherhood. The women are no longer mere hosts, but birth scenes show their painful participation in a process not of their making.[45] Laura Tisdall has contextualized the action of this novel within the developmental norms of the period, which were repeatedly challenged by 'special' children in fiction and film.[46]

At every stage in the narrative, events are subjected to a rigorous analysis by Gayford, Zellaby and the local doctors and clerics, the latter tending to be the weakest. The first major issue to emerge is that of origins. What was the agency which made the women pregnant? The novel's title encourages us to consider the pregnancies as impregnations of a host, possibly of a different species, and accordingly Zellaby explicitly takes his cue from the Victorian biologist Thomas Henry Huxley by positing the latter's term of 'xenogenesis'. Huxley glosses the term as signifying the 'generation of something foreign' and explores cases of species 'producing offspring which are of a totally different character from themselves'.[47] This term was later used by the American SF novelist Octavia E. Butler for her Xenogenesis Trilogy of novels exploring species limits and differences.[48] Beyond its suggestion of species difference, in Wyndham's novel the term 'xenogenesis' leaves origins unknown. Zellaby functions as the main intellectual commentator throughout the novel. Working on a study to be called *The British Twilight*, it is ironic that he doesn't survive the novel's conclusion.

Once the children are born, they are referred to variously as 'strangers', 'cuckoo-children' and 'changelings'. Gayford writes this othering into the text by designating them as the Children with a capital. In short, they are never accepted as normal members of their families, not simply because of the villagers' prejudice but because of alienating characteristics they display. They are quiet and unconventionally watchful. Their stare is noted again and again, especially from their gold-irised eyes. They are described as having an 'abstract foreignness' and resemble each other so closely that the girls can scarcely be distinguished from the boys. Through a simple behaviourist experiment, Zellaby demonstrates that anything learnt by one boy is shared by all the others and the same is true of the girls, implying a mass mind or collective consciousness, only separated on gender lines. On a more sinister level, they prove to have the capacity for telepathy, not only reading adults' minds but even controlling their actions from self-defence. When one local attempts to shoot one of the boys, he is induced to turn his gun on himself.

Once the Children's characteristics have been registered, Zellaby examines their implications, throwing out a clear allusion to George Bernard Shaw's *Back to Methuselah* (1921), a play which Wyndham cites in a 1954 essay as a prime example of the SF 'implicatory story'.[49] Zellaby speculates on evolutionary factors, citing the life force, superman and other issues. However, he isn't simply repeating Shaw's positions, but rather adopting a free-ranging intellectual voice similar to the latter's, in order to challenge the assumptions of his listeners, and by the same token Wyndham's readers. In particular he reaches a conclusion of evolutionary necessity where the authorities will have little choice but to kill the Children. This marks the culmination of an elaborate process of othering where the Children separate themselves from their 'families' and gather in the Grange. This refuge carries its own irony in that when the novel opens, covert experiments have been taking place there under the auspices of an unnamed 'Ministry'.[50]

The 1960 film adaptation as *Village of the Damned* differs from the novel in a number of respects.[51] Usually referred to as a 'horror movie', apart from omitting most of the discussions just referred to, it shows the Children as a much stronger visual presence. They are distinguished from the local children not only in their uniform hair colour, but also in their regimented dark clothes. And the film makes considerable play of their gaze closing up on their threatening stare as their pupils seem to radiate light. Through shot reverse shots, we see how their quasi-hypnotic effect on the humans is reflecting as a glazing of the latter's eyes prior to their submission. The Children are also given a much more substantial vocal presence. Many details of their actions in the novel come through reports, whereas now we see them in action and hear more from them. They seem more organized around David, the 'son' of the Zellabys, who engages in more of a dialogue with his 'father'. In the novel, however, late scenes show the Children speaking with the sobriety of adults and even echoing Zellaby in assertions like 'Sooner or later, you will try to kill us' (196) or the generalization that 'we are all [...] toys of the life-force' (200). One of the most dramatic scenes in the novel comes when one of the boys quietly and impassively challenges the male authority figures, and then induces a fit of sheer terror in the chief constable. As so often happens in the novel, the scene is charged with implications. If the Children can so easily defend themselves, how can they possibly be subdued?

The military intelligence source in the novel politicizes the subject when he reveals to the village that there have been other cases similar to the one unfolding in Midwich: one in a northern Australian village, another in a Canadian Eskimo settlement, and one in the Soviet Union near to Mongolia. We are given few details; suffice it that the children all perished in each case. The last example is the most ominous, however. In northern Russia, the authorities destroyed the whole village with a new 'experimental cannon'. Will this be the fate of Midwich? Or, to put it differently, how will the climax be represented? In a brief metafictional aside, Zellaby outlines how the scenario would play out in an American narrative with nationwide panic and a last-minute remedy from a scientific genius, whereas in Britain we encounter 'just another war' (187). Contrasting the Midwich situation with Wells's Martian invasion in *The War of the Worlds*, Zellaby insists that the danger is far greater in the former because there seems no way of countering the Children's telepathy. In the event he manages to smuggle explosives into the Grange and the novel ends with Gayford and his companions witnessing a massive explosion, presumably killing everyone there. The coda consists of lines from a note by Zellaby explaining the necessity of living by the laws of the jungle.

In 1961 Wyndham was approached by the company filming *Children of the Damned* to write a sequel to *The Midwich Cuckoos*. Despite his dislike of sequels, he briefly worked on one to be called *Midwich Main* – MGM's preferred title was *Tomorrow's Child*. In his draft Wyndham described how a boy is flown out of Russia carrying some of the characteristics of the Midwich children. The narrator is approached by British intelligence to gather details of similar cases from around the world. How that might have developed must remain speculation because by the end of 1961 Wyndham had abandoned the project.[52]

3

Permutations of
Science Fiction

THE OUTWARD URGE

In his later works Wyndham returned to a number of SF subjects and in every case presented his own variation on them. In 1959 he published a fix-up novel, *The Outward Urge*, as if written jointly with Lucas Parkes (another of Wyndham's pen names). Here the stories focused on the Troon family who were collectively subject, as one member explains, to 'a kind of urge onwards and outwards' into space (11). Wyndham modifies the more usual 'onwards and upwards', leaving it open whether the actions bring any improvement. In his *New Worlds* profile for April 1958, where the opening story first appeared, he explained that the Troon stories tried to be 'speculations not too far from the brink of possibility'.[1]

Wyndham's turn towards space travel might seem to mark a reversion to the themes of mainstream SF, but there is one historical factor to take into account here. On 4 October 1957, Russia launched Sputnik 1, the first artificial satellite to go into orbit around the Earth. The event triggered a wave of paranoia that the USA might be vulnerable to nuclear attack and marked one of the most critical moments in the Cold War.[2] Its impact on British SF was summed up by the editor of *New Worlds* John Carnell, who dated his editorial for November 1957 as 'Space Age, Year One', and who recorded the following year: 'At the moment there is a greatly increased interest in science fiction.[3]

British authors were quick to engage with the implications of the Sputnik launch. Peter Phillips's 'Next Step the Moon' (in *New Worlds*, January 1958) presented a montage of media reports and radio messages following the launch of a Soviet satellite whose astronauts are feared doomed. Arthur C. Clarke had of course been predicting communication satellites since 1945, but hastily revised two vignettes for publication in the wake of Sputnik. 'Special Delivery' presents space relays as a matter of course and dramatizes what happens when a freighter's autopilot jams; 'Freedom of Space' similarly evokes a world where satellite relays are already in place to describe the exhilaration of a space disc jockey at escaping the claustrophobia of American city life.[4] Unlike Wyndham's narratives, Clarke understates any political rivalry in interplanetary communication, concentrating instead on practical and technological problems which might arise. Wyndham himself, in a 1966 piece on Wells and SF, also registered the importance of Sputnik for the genre: 'It took a nasty body-blow when the first sputnik went up, it will take still more until it is gradually driven to practice in regions too remote to hold popular interest, and loses itself in the pursuit of novelty'.[5] We shall see how Wyndham takes an ironic and critical perspective on the whole enterprise of space exploration.

The opening sections of *The Outward Urge* were first published in *New Worlds* for 1958, two with titles taken from Rupert Brooke's 1908 poem 'The Jolly Company'. Wyndham draws on this poem to evoke the emptiness of space (the title of the last section), its sheer extent and the problems of communication. The final titles for the volume offer a trajectory of space exploration, with 50-year gaps, up to the final bleak coda. The sequence opens with a Troon member being interviewed for a post to help assemble a space station. Although the section is dated 1994, the contents of the interview reflect the position of Britain in the 1950s as the de facto junior partner of America in what had become known as the space race. Sputnik has already become history thanks to the enterprise of the 'Other Fellows' as the Russians are known: 'the Americans stole their thunder by making the first announcement on satellites. But they got their own back by putting the first one into orbit' (15).

Wyndham pays far more attention to how space is being conceptualized than giving the reader details of instruments and weapons. When we follow the protagonist up to the space station, or 'hulk' as it is known, the dimensions of space – 'thousands of miles of nothing' (17) – give an austere context to the work of construction. New norms of behaviour have become established, and Troon settles into that temporary routine before he returns to Earth. Until, that is, the sudden appearance of an unidentified flying object heading for the station. One problem the crew has is how to classify this 'half-missile, half-mine' (27) but the radio guidance is to treat it as hostile. Initially the missile strikes a very glancing blow at the station, severing Troon's anchor line, and so they appear to have had a lucky escape. Using his hand-tubes, Troon manages to land on the missile, riding its nose in an image which anticipates the climax of the 1964 film *Dr. Strangelove*, where a character rides a nuclear bomb to his doom. Troon's plan was to disable the missile's guidance system, but what the station commander actually sees in a sudden shift of perspective from near to far is 'a vivid, silent flash shining for its brief moment as brightly as the sun' (42). The sudden disappearance of Troon and missile is conveyed in terms recalling J. Robert Oppenheimer's description of the first atomic detonation as being 'brighter than a thousand suns'.[6] Although Wyndham slightly offsets Troon's sudden atomization with the news that he now has a son on Earth, this hardly softens the irony that his death was almost certainly caused by another human agency.

In 'The Moon: A.D. 2044', Michael Troon has become the commander of a station on that planet and war has broken out between the superpowers on Earth. Once again Wyndham opens his narrative with a dialogue, one more extended and probing than before, between Troon and the female doctor of the station. Her role is to interrogate Troon's beliefs and to question his authority by pointing to an incipient mutiny about to take place on the station. She also diagnoses a collective pathology of fatalistic estrangement gripping all the staff, and Troon feeds a similar critical awareness into his perceptions of the Moon, which is described as a void: 'there was only the impersonal savagery of nature, random, eternal, frozen, and senseless' (47). Allusions to Rupert Brooke are now supplemented by references to *Idiot's Delight*, Robert E. Sherwood's 1936 play which presents a group of characters in an Italian Alpine hotel gathered as a world war breaks out. Both the play and Wyndham's narrative explore distanced witness, since in the latter a nuclear war has broken out.

Space stations have by now become a reality: the Russians possess two, the British one, and the Americans one described as 'massive'. Information has been flagged up as crucial in the first story, but now it is conspicuous by its absence. Dr Ellen summarizes the launching of missiles by each side, but bitterly stresses how ignorant they are on the Moon base: 'All we *do* know for sure is that the two greatest powers there have ever been are out to destroy one another with every weapon they possess' (53). Wyndham does not allow any grand narrative of progress to take shape, instead evoking a situation where the staff of the Moon station are hovering on the verge of mental collapse. And all this is set within a context of national rivalries leading to a kind of space colonialism.

As in the opening story, dramatic tension mounts when two UFOs are seen heading for the Moon station. These turn out to be Russian 'platforms' seeking refuge after their own station has been destroyed. Apart from the launch of conventional missiles, the Russian station was attacked by miniature devices referred to as 'wasps', a kind of early drone weapon. The last section of the story gives an extended dialogue between Troon and the Russian general, who tells him how the war has developed from his point of view. It is he who summarizes the situation by declaring their common knowledge: 'We have all known in our hearts that this war, if it should come, would not be a kind that anyone could win'. (92) While it seems that everyone's fate is sealed, the story ends on a note of wishful thinking for rocket ships brining rescue. Troon declares: 'They'll come' (93).

That hope persists, but more tenuously, in 'Mars: A.D. 2094', which opens with a monologue from a Brazilian member of the Troon family having established a station on Mars. As happens throughout this volume, his thoughts have revolved around death so insistently that he is reduced to uncertainty about the reception of his 'log', as he calls his narrative. The latter is even directed towards a notional reader as offering evidence of his sanity. The reason for this anxiety is that the Great Northern War has taken place, a cataclysm reduced to one brief paragraph:

All over North America, all over Europe, all over the Russian Empire there were flashes that paled the sun, heat-waves that seared and set on fire whole countrysides. Monstrous plumes were writhing up into the sky, shedding ashes, dust, and death. (97)

The sheer speed and extent of the war suggests that there can be no winner and sets up a context where the persistence of the space programme seems absurd and futile. Nevertheless Trunho has managed to reach the red planet, but, as with the Moon, its landscape is featureless and void. From his perspective 'the meeting of sand and sky was marked by a thin dark line' (107), and that is all we are told.

The total absence of detail blocks us from seeing Mars as any kind of territorial prize. In fact Wyndham's evocation of the nuclear destruction of the northern hemisphere clearly draws on Nevil Shute's recent novel *On the Beach* (1957), where survivors of a nuclear war gather near Melbourne. In Wyndham's text we are told that 'Australia is the centre of the surviving British' (99), so here too the colony has become the sovereign state. However, the strongest irony emerges when we learn that in the regrouping of South America, Brazil devises a plan not only to rescue the British Moon station but also to secure 'its annexation, together with that of the entire Lunar Territory, to the Estados Unidos do Brasil' (100). Fuelled by imperial revenge, Brazil has revived its title as the First Republic to take over the Moon as its colony, unaware of the total lack of imperial commodities like wood and sugar which underpinned its original colonization.

Wyndham says little about the planning and execution of the Brazilian moonshot, concentrating instead on the dialogues between Trunho and his radio operator Camilo. Soon after they land, the spaceship topples over, injuring the latter and throwing Trunho back into the 'fear that has no cause, shape, or centre' (109). Once Camilo regains consciousness, he begins to hallucinate that Trunho is a Martian and the narrative shifts into a psychodrama between the two men, each trying to hide their real fears of the other. Finally, Camilo takes advantage of Trunho being outside the spaceship and attempts to launch it, but the vessel crashes, still intact, but killing Camilo. The bleak endpoint thus comes with Trunho in total isolation, fantasizing over the transmission of a letter to his loved one.

'*Venus*: A.D. 2144' continues the theme of colonial emptiness, moving to the misty, shifting Venusian landscape with shifting glimpses of reeds and trees, virtually a monochrome study of a water-bound world. Wyndham moves the perspective back to that of a main-branch member of the Troons, and the narrative returns to the more detached third person. Brazil has now grotesquely inflated its imperial ambitions through the slogan 'Space is a Province of Brazil', but their claim to Venus has been pre-empted by an Australian spaceship establishing a station on that planet. Caught between the options of direct attack and leaving the Australians in situ, the Brazilians assemble a latter-day armada headed by a spaceship called the 'Santa Maria', named after a town in southern Brazil and former site of imperial tension between Spain and Portugal. No sooner have the vessels landed than the Portuguese commander reveals that he has taken over the ship, explaining that the Brazilian Space Force 'was shot through with disaffection' (166). And so the expected conflict never materializes. When Troon suggests absurdly that the outcome could be used to declare that 'space has become a State of Australia', the Brazilian commander retorts that 'space will declare itself an independent territory' (167), apparently moving the debate into a postcolonial phase, but only by ignoring issues of territory and populus.

The coda to this sequence (added in 1961) is a sketch with the title '*The Emptiness of Space*: THE ASTEROIDS A.D. 2194', set not in space but on an island in New Caledonia, which at the time of publication was an overseas territory of France. In Wyndham's narrative the archipelago has achieved de facto independence with the destruction of Europe, but has allowed the creation of rocket base to be used by the newly independent 'Space', an entity which Wyndham never really explains. Now the narrator is an Australian visiting the town of Lahua (probably based on La Foa), where he meets the former rocket pilot George Troon, who has been so traumatized by the emptiness of space that he lives there as a recluse. We learn that another family member has piloted a rocket to the Asteroid Belt, where it is hit by a smaller rocket containing the corpse of the commander from Mars we encountered in the third story, a coincidence necessary to explain how the log in the latter reaches Earth. The sequence closes with characters commenting on how this Troon member is going through an extended living death.

With the possible exception of the coda, the stories in *The Outward Urge* have an austere consistency in repeatedly questioning the value of the space programme. The volume's title names an impulse, not a goal, and the stories constantly undercut any material gains from space voyages, focusing instead on their risks for the astronauts and the different ways in which the politics of Earth continue to be played out.

TROUBLE WITH LICHEN

Trouble with Lichen (1960) returns us to British society and the impact of discovering a substance that might retard the ageing process. The novel starts with an ending. In a brief opening scene, the funeral of a character called Diana is described as a carefully orchestrated Catholic ritual, with press coverage which includes brief reference to the death of an early suffragette. And there Wyndham leaves the preamble to the novel. The action proper opens with a beginning: a graduation celebration at a girls' school where the most promising student emerging into adult life is identified as one Diana Brackley. This scene is visualized by one of her teachers and it immediately establishes a characteristic which will inform the whole novel, namely that the vast majority of characters are female and that the action constantly interrogates the social roles then available to women in English society.

Diana herself plays a major part in this process. Her family background is of minimal importance, far less than the choice she faces between following the conventional route into marriage or developing her mind in further study. Amy Binns has rightly stressed the importance at this stage of his career of Wyndham presenting strongly assertive female protagonists, but the novel contextualizes this at every point within the general social options open to women.[7] Diana thus goes to Cambridge and then decides to pursue biochemistry under Dr Saxover, signing up for a research position at his private centre, Darr House Developments.[8] Here Diana and Saxover separately discover a lichen apparently possessing the power to retard the ageing process. Saxover immediately conceals the discovery while Diana develops this substance, realizing that it could constitute 'one of the most valuable, and explosive, secrets in the world' (41). After months of research, she leaves Darr House.

After a time gap of 14 years, we rejoin Saxover and his two youthful-looking children – a key detail because, unbeknown to them, he has been covertly administering Antigerone, as the new anti-ageing substance is known. In the meantime, we also learn that Diana has set herself up as director of an upper-class London-based beauty institute called Nefertiti Ltd. It is Saxover who indicates the links between their discovery and the long-standing dream of longevity when he imagines the promotional slogan 'You, Too, Can Be Methuselah!' (58), but it is Diana who implicitly links their activities to Bernard Shaw's 1921 play *Back to Methuselah*, a work which Wyndham greatly respected in the context of modern science fiction. In his elaborate set of prefaces, Shaw speculates on voluntary longevity and creative evolution, an attempt to harmonize evolution with the creative impulse first popularized by Henri Bergson in his 1907 *Creative Evolution*. In a similar spirit Diana speculates to Saxover's daughter Zephanie that her father and she have found a 'step in evolution, a kind of synthetic evolution – and the *only* evolutionary advance by man in a million years' (85). Although she originally planned to gather a group of utopian pioneers, her ambitions have taken a more commercial turn in setting up a new business.

Diana's successful commercialization of her discovery coincides with a shift in the second half of the novel to social commentary. The discovery and development of the eponymous lichen constitutes its element of science fiction, but in Parts 2 and 3 Wyndham explores the social dynamic of how the news of the discovery leaks into the public sphere. More and more attention is devoted to the styles of news reporting, the newspapers' use of delaying climaxes or innuendoes, for example. And throughout, Diana's remains the most articulate commenting voice, as when she dons the guise of anthropologist to declare: 'the present primary social role of western woman is as wife; her secondary status is as mother; in upper and middle classes her tertiary status is sometimes that of companion' (116). As the interest in the product grows, Diana uses the girls on her staff to plant red herrings in the press that she is actually using Irish seaweed in her company, in order to sound out public opinion. In short, apart from her research, she combines the skills of promoter, investigator and even manipulator of public opinion. Furthermore, Diana's actions help focus the novel's whole scrutiny of the relation between gender, the ageing process and ideas of the future.[9]

As the novel develops, through pastiche 'excerpts', Wyndham focuses more and more closely on the styles of named newspapers and the narrative shifts into an extended montage sequence, jumping from a message to the home secretary, a dialogue between women and an exchange between a doctor and a female patient about her age. The effect resembles a cinematic newsreel of fragments from different social areas. We are given a glimpse of an official speculating on informing the Queen, suddenly followed by a dialogue in a London pub to convey the social spread of concern with the Antigerone. There is even a brief excerpt from Radio Moscow. And Diana herself gets caught up in the media frenzy when she manages to wrong-foot an interviewer from the BBC. Indeed, throughout the second half of the novel the media occupy the foreground.

Towards the end of the novel there is a steady rise in the drama of public reaction to the Antigerone. Zephanie and her fiancé are kidnapped at gunpoint and the latter beaten until she reveals the origins of the lichen. A crisis breaks out in the stock market as one company after another refuses payments to anyone taking the substance. Saxover's centre is burnt to the ground and Diana is shot and killed as she leaves her building – or is she? In the coda she meets Saxover at her new home and they agree to a secret marriage. Has Diana finally succumbed to convention? The science fiction subject is not closed off because she has hidden samples of the lichen. As usual with Wyndham, the door is left ajar to further developments.

CHOCKY

Chocky (1968) was Wyndham's last novel to be published in his lifetime and is one which weaves new variations on the SF theme of alien possession which often fed into the paranoia of the Cold War. Robert Heinlein's *The Puppet Masters* (1951) describes how slug-like organisms from outer space latch on to the backs of humans and direct their actions, while the 1956 film *The Invasion of the Body Snatchers* shows how extraterrestrial buds can create simulacra of their human victims which are identical to their originals except for their wooden emotionless manner. In these narratives the invading agent comes from elsewhere, is unknown, controlling its subjects in ways difficult to identify and therefore rationalized as illness.

Wyndham avoids virtually all of these features by setting up his narrative as a family drama, where the twelve-year-old son Michael begins to behave strangely and is witnessed speaking to an unseen companion. The narrator is Michael's adoptive father, distanced from his birth but thereby well positioned to observe him and try to understand what is happening to him. An implicit analogy emerges between Michael's behaviour and that of his stepsister Polly, who has a fantasy companion called Piff that she converses with. Piff is introduced as an analogy with Matthew's companion and is one of the first signs of a strategy which Wyndham follows throughout the novel. At every point where something mysterious happens to Michael, his parents, teachers and doctors attempt to analyse developments by drawing analogies with other children's behaviour. Thus it is accepted as normal for a young child to keep company with a fantasy figure in her imagination, and if it's not strange for Polly, why should it be strange for Michael? There is, however, their difference in names. 'Piff' can serve as an English slang term for 'good', whereas, as Margaret Atwood has pointed out, the name of Michael's companion, Chocky, carries no implication of gender, suggests diminutive size, and could be read as a slang contraction of 'chocolate', or alternatively as a form of 'chokey' or 'time in prison'.[10] Piff is taken to be female, and Chocky is usually gendered as female although there are no definite signs of gender. More importantly, the narrator tells us about Piff as if she were a real companion, but in a tongue-in-cheek way as if humouring his daughter's imagination.

Poised between childhood and adolescence, Michael could therefore be sharing his sister's fantasy life, or alternatively something else could be happening, and it is this unspecified possibility which stays with us throughout the novel. The first one-sided conversation we witness is one where Matthew is insisting on the number of hours in a day and days in a week as if these standard measurements were being questioned by his interlocutor. Significantly there is no suggestion of threat here, only of strange questioning. Matthew's replies set the tone for subsequent conversations between the adults about his behaviour, where all are seeking to contain its strangeness within social and cultural norms. There is also a metafictional dimension to the early episodes as if the narrator was composing a character with the other members of the family. Thus we are told that 'Chocky quite markedly lacked physical attributes. He/she appeared to be scarcely more than a presence, having perhaps something in common with Wordsworth's cuckoo' (27). The reference here is to Wordsworth's poem 'To the Cuckoo', where he addresses the bird as a disembodied companion, a voice at large. The narrative is implicitly contextualized (and to a certain extent normalized) within the Romantic tradition of English literature. Matthew's father still has reservations, however, about his 'trick' of posing as interlocutor between Chocky and others. 'Trick' could suggest an intention to deceive, but Matthew appears to be genuinely puzzled by Chocky because he does talk rather like a boy' (30), but not about the subjects which would engage one. As tensions within the family mount, Mary the mother shows increasing anxiety about what is happening to Matthew. Ironically, she articulates one of the central themes of the novel when she declares that 'reality is relative' (34), but uses this conviction to attempt to control Matthew's behaviour through unspecified therapy.

Wyndham gradually opens up the subject of Matthew to more and more people, not least at his school, where his maths teacher assumes that he has been receiving help in his studies. A dialogue with his father demonstrates his easy skill with binary maths, for example. This and similar events cue in his request for assistance from a psychotherapist called Landis, who serves as one of the main commentators in the novel. It is Landis who raises, and then dismisses, the notion that Matthew's case resembles 'possession', which Wyndham had already touched on in *The Midwich Cuckoos*, as if 'Chocky is a wandering, if not a wanton, spirit that has invaded Matthew' (57). Landis's role in the novel is clearly to articulate possibilities that might have occurred to the reader and to dismiss them. At the same time, however, he registers real curiosity about the boy's case, which does not fit any pattern he knows. As if to confirm his puzzlement, soon after his first discussion of Matthew, the boy begins to paint pictures where the human figures are elongated, as if normal visual perception was not operating. Landis suggests a thoughtful open-minded attitude to Matthew's behaviour, in comic contrast with the family doctor who recommends plenty of exercise and a daily cold shower.

Matthew's case attracts considerable public attention when, during a family holiday on the Welsh coast, he saves the life of his sister Polly when she falls into the water. News spreads to the local, then national newspapers, with Matthew even being interviewed on BBC radio. In the latter the interviewer tries to play up the mystery of the event but the interview supports Matthew's credibility in demonstrating his awareness of how strange his experience was, but also his care over describing it. 'Guardian angel' is a handy label for the media, though one dismissed by a 'dotty old clergyman' (103). These details serve as an important preamble to his disappearance soon afterwards for several days. Once again, appearances are deceptive. It sounds as if Matthew has been abducted, but after his return he explains that he has been in hospital recovering from an accident. Yet again his father carefully explains that for clarity he has tried to exclude the boy's hesitations, but the story remains enigma.

It seems as if Matthew's problem has passed when he explains that Chocky has left, but this proves to be only temporary. She/ he returns and expresses the desire to speak to his father, who carefully introduces that scene by stressing that 'there was no air of séance about it, nothing of the medium about Matthew' (138–9). There is, however, a flatness of delivery suggesting the voice of another, and the utterances initially are punctuated with gestures of clarification ('I mean'). At this point Wyndham's novel approaches most closely to science fiction, but Chocky avoids the clichés of the genre by simply stating that his/her people come from 'far away', do rarely travel in spaceships, and that their life is under threat.[11] Although Chocky recognizes the existence of Earthly intelligence, it is still very limited and the whole notion of progress is taken to task, partly because it doesn't recognize the importance of radiation as an infinite power source. Chocky speaks critically, but not threateningly, emphasizing the prime need of respecting life: 'Intelligent forms are rare. In each form they owe a duty to all other forms. Moreover, some forms are complementary. No one can assess the potentialities that are latent in any intelligent form' (144). Wyndham draws on the traditional identification of an extraterrestrial world as older than Earth (especially in references to Mars) and presents a series of general truths on a high level of abstraction, all of which pulls against Chocky's supposed youth. The key to the message cannot be verbalized and is simply indicated as 'xxxxx', a cryptic cypher which might indicate meaning.

Chocky's message to the narrator (and of course the reader) is the only one being offered. It clarifies that some alien consciousness occupied Matthew, but there is a new twist to the narrative which moves its focus off the boy and on to something rather more sinister. Earlier in the novel Matthew is sent to a Harley Street psychotherapist, who puts the boy under hypnosis and then gives a cursory Freudian interpretation of the swimming event, i.e. that the crisis unblocked his resistance to swimming. However, although Matthew was under hypnosis, Chocky wasn't, and was able to register all his actions. Particularly Chocky registers all the tricks tried by Sir William 'to invent, or to lie, with misleading questions' (147). The fact that he fails excites him so much that he registers the fact by phoning others – presumably his superiors. Next he administers drugs to test him further and, as Chocky states, 'they wrung him dry. Every detail, every word I had ever told him went into their tape-recorders' (148). Chocky's last words in the novel relocate the threat from the alien to the 'power-empires' on Earth, with which the establishment figure Sir William appears to be collaborating. It appears as if Matthew has been unwittingly drawn into some kind of covert mind-control experiment and at that point the narrative ends.

WEB

Web (1979), first published ten years after Wyndham's death, combines two SF themes: the utopia and a Darwinian species drama. It opens with the admission that the project about to be described was a complete failure. Narrated by Arnold Delgrange, who loses his family in a traffic accident, the novel recounts the story of the purchase of a Pacific island by the wealthy Lord Foxfield in order to establish a 'free, independent community endowed with the opportunity, and the means, to create a new climate of living'.[12] In short, it will be a utopian community experimenting with social improvement. The narrative includes allusions to H. G. Wells's 1923 novel *Men Like Gods*, which describes the transposition of a group of British characters into a distant future where utopia appears to have been realized in a society free from conflict. Ironically the figures from the reader's present actually introduce conflict into the action, which brings into question the very possibility of realizing such a society. However, there is a fundamental difference between the landscapes in *Men Like Gods* and *Web*, which suggests that Wyndham was working within quite a different genre. In Wells, the world of the future is depicted within a temperate, largely rural landscape. The latter has no historical dimension and functions instead as an emblematic representation of its utopian society, whereas from the very beginning Wyndham situates his own project within the complex history of western colonialism. Foxfield himself sets a negative tone when he defines humanity exclusively in power terms as the 'mightiest species', apparently free to act in any way they feel able. The narrative of *Web* traces out in miniature a series of checks and challenges to the arrogance of this species.

Delgrange introduces Foxfield's project ironically through a series of literary allusions which suggest that it was naively fantastic, even though Foxfield himself denies that it involves a 'lotus-land, an Eden, or even a utopia' (18). These allusions suggest that it is a dream (*The Tempest*), an attempt to create a New Age (Shelley's 'Hellas' chorus), or an illusion of self-empowerment (W. E. Henley's poem 'Invictus' with its stirring declaration 'I am the Master of my fate'). More importantly, Delgrange references two novels which function as intertexts to *Web*. Addressing the members of his project, Foxfield declares: 'You are setting out to plant that seed in a brave new world' (18); and once the voyage to the Pacific is underway, Delgrange's companion Camilla foregrounds gender when she comments that '"Men like gods" is too tempting a target for the opposition' (58). Wyndham has reversed the order of influence here because Aldous Huxley explained that he had intended *Brave New World* to reveal the 'horrors of the Wellsian utopia' and, more specifically, that his novel had 'started out as a parody of H. G. Wells' *Men Like Gods*'.[13]

Wyndham distances his narrative from both novels by pursuing an issue neither includes – the history of the proposed site for Lord Foxfield's community. The fact that this is a Pacific island compounds Wyndham's ironies because it inevitably recalls another novel by Wells – *The Island of Doctor Moreau* (1896), where the scientist has avoided legal and social hostility towards vivisection by installing himself in a distant island which doubles as a laboratory and a quasi-colonial domain. Moreau's experiments rebound fatally on him, and right from the start of Delgrange's history the island is associated with death. The first party of western sailors to land on the island discover that it is inhabited but also find a cross commemorating the deaths of earlier sailors 'all et by the cannibal savidges' (26). Every detail of Delgrange's account heightens the anti-colonial ironies.[14] The islanders avoid 'protection', as imperial occupation is euphemistically called, and they experience a brief moment of pride in defeating a German garrison party. Fast forward to the 1950s and the natives debate whether to evacuate their island because, as the colonial governor explains, 'up out of the ocean there would come a great ball of fire brighter than a hundred suns' (35). Oppenheimer has earlier been listed in the great names of western technological progress and at this point, the novel's focus begins to shift from colonial occupation to ecological concerns.

The British colonial administration admit that the natives are the 'true owners' of the island, but the novel's focus switches here from the colonizer to the colonized to show internal disputes over whether to evacuate or not. Particular emphasis falls on the figure of Nokiki, who refuses to leave and, under the conviction that he is living through the 'end of an era', places a ritual curse on the island by appealing to the Maori judge-figure: 'He besought Nakaa to declare the island of Tanakuatua for-ever tabu to all men; to decree that if men should try to live on it they should sicken and die' (45). Shortly after the ritual, a British inspection party declares the island to be completely 'clean' after the nuclear tests. We thus have rival versions of the island presented – as cursed or healthy – and after this extended preamble the party arrives to establish Foxfield's community.

The first impressions of the island on the narrator and his scientist companion Camilla are positive but challenging, and also complicated by the legacy of the nineteenth century. Delgrange expresses a Darwinian view of 'all those plants fighting one another for existence' (62). This is then countered by Camilla who expresses the strongest perspective on the island's life: 'Nature is a process, not a state – a continuous process. A striving to keep alive. No species has a *right* to exist; it simply has ability, or the inability' (64).[15] Her austere warning even applies to the politics of the island, which the preamble has shown to be in constant historical flux. Two characteristics of the island stand out to the observers: the absence of birds and patches of mist hanging among the trees. A member of the group runs into one of the patches of mist and is shortly after found dead with a 'vivid scarlet' face. It is Camilla who realizes that the 'mist' is a dense cloud of spider webs, and here we should turn to a third text by Wells which probably suggested his subject to Wyndham.

'The Valley of Spiders' (1903) describes three men pursuing fugitives across an unspecified wild landscape when they encounter large balls or 'globes' which they can't identify and even the shape is fluid: 'it was not an even sphere at all, but a vast, soft, ragged filmy thing, a sheet gathered by the corners, an aerial jelly-fish, as it were, but rolling over and over as it advanced, and trailing long, cobwebby threads and streamers that floated in its wake'. These entities pose a conceptual threat in being impossible to identify, and then a physical threat when they attack one of the pursuers: 'he had the impression of many eyes, of a dense crew of squat bodies, of long, many-jointed limbs hauling at their mooring ropes to bring the thing down upon him'.[16] Wells plays on the perceptual flux caused by near and far perspectives. The 'globes' can scarcely be seen, let alone resisted. In fact, their threat is localized in the valley of the title, whereas in *Web* the 'mists' seem to have conquered the whole island. Wyndham follows Wells's cue in disrupting our association of spiders with the ground. But can spiders fly? objects Delgrange. Once again Camilla gives the most cogent reply, citing Darwin's *Voyage of the Beagle*, where in Chapter 8 he describes a 'flocculent web' of spiders which had landed on his boat.

Just as Camilla challenges Delgrange to revise his perceptions of nature, Wyndham uses 'web' as a catch-all term of connectedness, inviting the reader to consider relations between the natives and the terrain, between the island and the outside world. Delgrange's first impression of the island is of 'romantic tourist literature come to life' (59), soon dispelled by the first death in their group, and throughout the novel Wyndham takes care to challenge the potential clichés in his narrative. One such would be the relationship between Delgrange and Camilla. As a character she is given very little physical description and comes across primarily as an alert and realistic voice constantly correcting Delgrange's presumptions. However, even when they are taken captive by the natives and forced to remove their clothes, there is no suggestion of any kind of sexual bond between them. Her role is primarily to clarify the implications of the central subject. They have earlier witnessed the species war in miniature when a cloud of spiders settles on a crab and kills it. Camilla later explains how spiders' behaviour shows a group intelligence at work, perhaps indicating the 'beginning of a revolution; the beginning of a takeover of power' (101), blurring the boundary between their actions and human behaviour.

This process starts with the reversal of the assumption by Foxfield's group that their island is simply a location that can be used for their own purposes. Having identified the extraordinarily coordinated actions of the spiders, Delgrange and Camilla are taken captive by the dissident islanders who refused the evacuation, led by a man who sports a 'childlike representation of a spider' on his chest; 'childlike' suggesting a codified representation and also the colonial infantilization of a subject race. They are ordered to remove their clothes, not so much to humiliate them as to ensure that they are not concealing weapons, and then are taken to a settlement containing an 'arrangement of stones' – to be sacrificed? In fact the leader Naeta only obliges them to listen to his own counter-narrative of trickery by the imperial authorities. His account nullifies the 'purchase' of the island on which the utopian project was based. Prior to Naeta's story, Camilla and Delgrange have been led unscathed through patches of spiders and they realize that the islanders have identified an oil which acts as a repellent.

Most of Naeta's story is filtered through Delgrange, who admits to confusion when recording it. However, his account has a clear logic as in the following sequence: 'it was only right that the Government who had tricked them into leaving the island, and so was responsible for the curse that was put on it, should find them another place to live, but that did not mean that they had *sold* their island' (116). Naeta distinguishes between control and ownership, and places the responsibility for the curse squarely with the colonial authorities. Furthermore, he surprises Camilla by claiming a relation to the spiders by naming them as his 'Little Sisters', literally springing into being from his father's remains, thereby disturbing the Darwinian species rigidity Delgrange and Camilla have been applying. The latter has named the local spider species *Araneus nokikii* in an act of intellectual possession worthy of a nineteenth-century naturalist, although they have probably mutated from the radiation of the local bomb tests. The novel undermines empire by setting up a range of counter-voices from Naeta and his companions that rival those of the colonial administrators.[17] This strategy could further be related to Wyndham's constant reversals of perspective and implicitly bear yet again on the novel's title, which suggests a complex network of connections.

Despite the racialized expectations of violence and even murder, the two return unscathed to their settlement, where they live under siege until finally rescued. It is as if they are under constant observation: 'They stood packed as closely as pebbles on a beach, and as motionless. To the eye alone they were inert enough to be dead [...] Something more than sight, too, which gave a sense of thousands of eyes watching one, alert for the moment' (131). Traditionally in 'castaway' narratives the return to the home civilization gives closure and the reestablishment of normality, but Wyndham avoids closure with a brief coda that an example of the island spider species has been found in Peru, as if the species might be escaping into the outer world. And so, yet again, in *Web* Wyndham ironizes an attempt to set up a utopia as ignorant, ill-informed and doomed to failure.

4

Consider Her Ways and Other Stories

In 1946 John Carnell founded the SF journal *New Worlds* which, after some initial difficulties, became one of the leading media for publishing SF in Britain. From 1948 to 1954 Wyndham (as John Beynon Harris) served as a director of its parent company Nova Publications. In his first editorial Carnell declared a range of subjects which implicitly reflected on the unpredictability of his own enterprise: 'from here on, then future looms as a bewildering Land of If, governed by the whims and passions of individuals, by the power of Governments, by the discoveries of scientists, even by the failures and catastrophes which beset us'.[1] As if in ironic confirmation of Carnell's uneasy evocation of the future, the readership of *New Worlds* grew dramatically after the atomic bomb was dropped on Hiroshima. Brian Aldiss dismissed *New Worlds* until Michael Moorcock took over the editorship in 1964 as 'operating like an outpost of the American pulp tradition', but this is to ignore Carnell's editorial policy.[2] His purpose was to establish a British-based SF journal and to this end he took fiction by Arthur C. Clarke, John Christopher, Wyndham – as we shall see in a moment – and, further into the 1950s, younger writers like Aldiss himself and J. G. Ballard, whose editorial profile recorded that he was 'interested' in Wyndham's work.[3] In 1951 Carnell organized an International Science Fiction Convention in London, where Wyndham was an active participant, and in a 1956 editorial he spelt out explicitly his national emphasis, declaring that 'British authors will almost always produce stories written differently (in style and presentation), from American writers, around plots approached from a different angle, a direct result of different environments, customs and conditions, existing in the two countries'.[4] It was key to Carnell's strategy for him to publish this fiction so as to establish SF in the British market.

Wyndham began contributing to *New Worlds* as early as the second issue in October 1946, still writing as John Beynon. 'The Living Lies', described in an editorial header as a 'beautifully-written psychological story', is set in a future when Venus has been colonized and settled. Primarily that planet used as a distanced setting for an alternative society rigidly colour-coded between Whites, Greens, Reds and Blacks. The story opens abruptly when Leonie Ward, a White girl recently arrived on Venus, accidentally runs down and kills one of a group of Green girls in the city. She is rescued from what could become a race riot and then is gradually educated by her companion in the racial make-up of Venus. The Whites are in control of the hospitals and to further their exploitation of the planet they have fabricated a system of race where newly born children are administered a colouring grease made permanent by a 'projector' machine. The purpose of the colouring is to create tensions between racial groups. As Leonie learns, 'it's the old, old game. Make the people distrust one another, keep them at loggerheads, prevent them from uniting for their rights and you can rule'.[5] Being a newcomer, Leonie knows nothing about Venus society and (like the reader) is given a serial exposition of how the whole concept of race has been separated from physical actuality and transformed into arbitrary colouring for the purposes of divide and control.

Outraged by this account, Leonie begins questioning different groups without realizing that her actions are being monitored by the secret police. Her companion and 'instructor', himself masquerading as a Green, realizes her danger and insists that her only defence lies in a similar disguise as she too becomes a Green. As she gazes in the mirror at her new self-image, the result is startling alienation:

> A face with a complexion soft and velvet, but green as grass. The lips, after the manner of most Green women, were painted a brilliant red, they matched the small rings in her ears. There was a faint shading of dusky powder on her eyelids which was also a fashion among Green women [...] This was herself. This thing in the mirror.[6]

The features which estrange Leonie are those added with the cosmetics as well as the superimposed new colouring. In her naivete she hopes that she can start a revolutionary movement, especially when she learns of another projector machine which can reverse the effects of the first. However, an experiment to demonstrate this breaks down into the chaos of a race riot where Leonie is lynched. The last speakers in the narrative are members of the secret police and so the regime stays intact at the end of this austerely Orwellian tale published almost three years before *Nineteen Eighty-Four* was published.

It was a measure of the importance Wyndham attached to *New Worlds* that in 1955 he edited a collection of the best fiction from that magazine. His introduction sets the latter in the context of the postwar period with all its attendant shortages of paper and funding, but particularly in contrast with the SF scene in America. He recorded that 'in the United States there was a boom in science fiction, but no British publishing house seemed to perceive it', until, that is, the foundation of *New Worlds*, which took place against a background threat of a 'transatlantic deluge of well-fed glossies and bulky pulps'.[7] Wyndham outlines the difficulties the journal experienced until it achieved stability of production by the mid-1950s and he stresses that it was 'founded upon the theory that science fiction is capable of dealing with matters of more general interest than cosmic cowboys and galactic gunmen' (12).

More broadly than applied in this particular periodical, Wyndham uses his introduction to reflect on the general characteristics of science fiction, probing behind the generic label (which he deplored for most of his career), which suggests 'super space-ships and galactic warfare'. To bolster his argument, he draws an analogy with the 'intelligent detective story' which 'finds entertainment in the posing and logical solution of a problem'. He continues: 'now, good science fiction differs from galactic gallivanting by doing just this. It asks: "What would happen if ...?" It puts the proposition forward in story form, and then does its best to answer it'. At this point Wyndham stresses the parallels in method between detective fiction and SF:

> Both forms are exploiting the fascination of logical deduction; and in both, the reader, pitted against the writer, is looking for holes in

the argument, or errors upon which he can pounce with a cry of triumph. The differences between the two are, in fact much more apparent than real: they lie chiefly in the décor, and the wider terrain over which the game is played, and in requiring a different background knowledge from the reader [...] The rules for the two forms are not, of course, quite the same, but they are both based upon the same fundamental concept – that there is an imagined situation which is to be resolved within the chosen frame, by logical probability. (11–12)

Right up to the end of his career Wyndham was constantly re-examining the nature of the SF genre and differentiating its sensational popular features from its potential for serious narration. His analogy with detective fiction helps domesticate SF by playing down the extraordinary, a strategy which fits well with Carnell's editorial policy for *New Worlds*. Wyndham's methodological comparisons also take implicit bearings from his own early crime fiction and shed light on the opening section of his novel *Plan for Chaos*.

Another SF magazine which Wyndham praised for impacting on the British market was *Science Fantasy*, founded in 1950 by Walter Gillings, who had worked with Wyndham before the war (see Chapter 1) and who edited it until taken over by John Carnell. In the editorial for the inaugural issue, Gillings declared: 'SCIENCE-FANTASY which is – intentionally – fiction. Science-fantasy which is – or might well be – fact. In this magazine we shall be concerned with it in all its forms'.[8] Diversity was to be the keynote. Contributors included Eric Frank Russell, John Brunner, Brian Aldiss and J. G. Ballard. Although the policy was to promote British authors, American writers like C. M. Kornbluth and Judith Merril were also included, as was Wyndham himself, with a story in the third issue called 'Pawley's Peepholes' (originally 'Operation Peep' 1951).

In his foreword to his 1956 story collection *The Seeds of Time*, Wyndham stressed the stories' diversity, explaining that he had selected those which were 'virtually experiments, made at intervals during fifteen years, in adapting the science-fiction motif to various styles of short story' (2). They were, in other words, selected to show the versatility of the genre and offered against the perceived dominance of the adventure story, particularly in the USA. Thus, 'Survival' (1952) counters the overwhelming masculine presence in space narratives by showing not just a young woman but one expecting a child joining a spaceship crew. After the vessel misfires and falls into orbit round Mars, a rescue ship finds her – the sole-survivor – singing to her baby, the very image of maternity. However, the story implies that she might have survived by consuming the bodies of her fellow astronauts. The stories collected in *The Seeds of Time* do have, however, a thematic coherence, indicated by the title of the collection, in mostly engaging with aspects of time. This can be seen in the opening story 'Chronoclasm' (in Greek 'time breaker;' see Ketterer 2013), which dramatizes a series of disruptions of the present by a visitor from the twenty-second century. It follows a Wellsian pattern of framing the invention of a 'history machine', i.e. a machine which facilitates access to history, within a 'common man' figure who turns scientist within our present. The disruptions are enacted by a young woman called Tavia (Octavia), who disrupts the mundane life of the narrator, eventually marrying him and who admits to idealizing the mid-twentieth century.[9] The burgeoning romance between her and the narrator takes second place to their dialogues about the supposed machine which makes her transitions possible. In the future they have become accepted devices, but under strict supervision with permits and with the absolute rule that time visitors can only observe, otherwise they would cause a 'chronoclasm', a disruption in time which might have unforeseen consequences. In effect, this is what happens when Tavia apparently helps the narrator to succeed in his award-winning scientific research.[10] At the end of the story she simply disappears and the narrative tails off with the narrator beginning to compose a message to the future Tavia. Fantasy? Attempted wish-fulfilment? The ambiguity is increased by the segmented nature of the text which constantly shows encounters at different moments in time, compelling the reader to assess their sequentiality.

The issue of planetary colonization also informs 'Time to Rest' (1949), another story to appear in *New Worlds* and to be collected in *The Seeds of Time*. Probably owing a debt to Ray Bradbury's *The Martian Chronicles* which Wyndham admired, it presents a figure called Bert who drifts round the waterways of Mars on a home-made boat, surviving precariously 'like a gypsy' on odd jobs picked up along the way. Wyndham follows the tradition of presenting Mars as an ancient world with a temperate climate and with well-established settlements by Earthmen. Although Wyndham describes the story as 'somewhat pastoral', the subject is far bleaker because Bert is not simply an itinerant, but also cut off from Earth, which has blown up into fragments, possibly from a nuclear disaster. He arrives at a 'stone cube' worn smooth by the passage of time, still in use as a dwelling, and meets a Martian family he is used to dealing with, specifically a local woman called Annika. Wyndham carefully specifies her skin colouring as 'reddish-brown', implicitly contextualizing the situation within the history of colonization. Bert rehearses the behaviour of Earthmen on that planet as collectively suffering from a 'trouble underneath': 'A number wandered restlessly as he did; most of them preferred to rot slowly and alcoholically in the settlements. A few, grasping at shadows while they dreamed, had taken Martian girls and tried to go native' (33). The latter option presents itself to Bert when he is attracted to a young girl in the family and is invited by Annika to move in with the family on a permanent basis. Though tempted, he rejects the offer because he would stay the 'Earthman', permanently estranged from the Martians. Wyndham's title is bleakly ironic because Bert has no home base of any kind and at the end of the story simply recedes from the narrative, presumably continuing to wander. 'Time to Rest' thus gives us yet another variation on one of Wyndham's most recurrent subjects, the death of empire.

In the same collection 'Meteor' revolves around the problematic relation of endings to fresh beginnings. First published in *Amazing Stories* for 1941 as 'Phoney Meteor', it was written originally with the Second World War in the immediate background, which added a particular irony to the story, which alternates between characters in the present examining a mysterious rock which falls out of the sky on the one hand, and on the other extracts from the journal of an extraterrestrial being who flees his dying planet. The characters in the present are concerned primarily with the practicalities of examining the rock, whereas the journal excerpts demonstrate a philosophical reflectiveness on the age and survival of culture, which is defined as follows: 'civilization is, from the beginning, the ability to coordinate and direct natural forces' (45). The former exist primarily in the present; the latter planetary travellers take their bearings from large stretches of time. The fact that the journal excerpts are introduced without any contextualization invites the reader to compare the two sequences which alternate until we realize that the group referred to in the journals are actually travelling to Earth in a 'globe' (suggesting a whole world) which the characters on Earth see simply as a rock.

The travellers are in flight from a dying world hoping to start their lives afresh on the 'blue, shining world' of Earth. In its original form the story sets up the bleak irony that their place of refuge should be ravaged by war. When revising the text Wyndham dropped all the topical allusions to air wardens and bombs which strengthened the ambiguity of the 'meteor', maybe as a secret weapon, and by so doing he lost that irony. In its place he retains the disparity in size between the two groups. The extraterrestrials are tiny beings, hence their surreal visual perspective on things of the Earth. A curious cat is described as a predatory monster who is killed with a 'fire-rod', but then more travellers lose their lives after being attacked by smaller monsters, probably rats. At the very end of the story humans have realized they are encountering tiny creatures (with a painful sting) who they wipe out by covering them in insecticide. Prior to this, the characters of Earth have managed to slice the 'ball' in half to reveal mini compartments of metal, 'packs of minute tubes, things that look like tiny seeds' and other objects which tease their curiosity.

Wyndham stresses a physical disparity of scale which pulls against the articulate language of the journals. The latter are kept by a character called Oss ('os' meaning 'mouth' in Latin) The fact that both texts – narrative and journals – are written in a common language ironically underlines their total lack of communication. To the travellers the creatures of Earth are monsters; to the latter the travellers are insects. Unusually the story carried an editorial postscript to its original version stating that it was

> the most significant story we have published, concerning space travel, and visitants from other worlds. Life on other planets is bound to be vastly different from life on our own world, and the chances of either one of the two forms of life recognizing the intelligence of the other is extremely remote indeed.[11]

The main obstacle to the travellers realizing a new life on Earth is not a 'natural force', but other supposedly intelligent beings and their hopes for a new beginning actually brings about their end.

'Pawley's Peepholes' is set in an American city where strange apparitions are seen – legs dangling from the ceiling of a concert hall, a disembodied head on a sidewalk. More and more cases are reported in the local press and the narrator draws a comparison with the prewar writings of Charles Fort which collected anomalous phenomena. His method 'was to labour mightily with scissors and paste, present the resulting collation, and leave it to a largely indifferent world to judge whether nearly everybody wasn't wrong about most everything'.[12] This method of collection is contrasted with that of the narrator's friend Jimmy, who collates all the viewings and locates a 'focus of disturbance'. At the same time the narrator and his partner actually experience one of these apparitions when a young lady in a pink tunic seems to step out of a brick wall. All three figures gaze at each other, then 'the girl opened her mouth as if she were speaking, but no sound came. Then she made a forget-it gesture, turned, and walked back into the wall' (8). There are no atmospherics, the gesture is familiar and then the event passes. The careful simplicity of the prose focuses our attention on the single incongruity of the woman's appearance and departure.

However, a second subject becomes more and more evident as the story progresses and the apparitions modulate into group images of a sales platform with the following banners:

PAWLEY'S PEEPHOLES ON THE PAST –

GREATEST INVENTION OF THE AGE

HISTORY WITHOUT TEARS FOR $10.00 (13)[13]

At such points it becomes evident that the apparitions could be part of a show mounted in the future, where for a fee customers are offered glimpses back into the narrator's present. The subject then approaches satire in the denouement where the city in the present out-does the future business in promotion. Where the future entrepreneurs attempt to shock the citizens of our present into perceiving their lives as an ongoing theatrical spectacle, the town now reverses this perspective by promoting the visitations as a 'Futurama Spectacle', with the result that they cease. The allusion here is to Norman Bel Geddis's exhibition at the New York World's Fair for 1939 which showed how the future life of American cities might develop. Wyndham's original title for this story was 'Operation Peep', but 'Pawley's Peepholes' better captures the commercial dimension to its novelty. The ultimate subject thus emerges as how the future could be represented and thereby commercialized, as if in one of Mark Twain's satires.

The programme of *Science Fantasy* was not only to publish fiction but also to promote the analysis of SF. The second number carried four essays discussing the pedigree of SF and space opera, among other topics, and in Spring 1954 Wyndham himself contributed a guest editorial on 'The Pattern of Science Fiction', discussed in Chapter 5. Apart from examining the general methods of SF, Wyndham also comments on the 'crassness of the illustrators who under the guidance of the money-in-sex publishers have evolved the convention of the brassiered and pantied cutie accompanying the space-suited hero'.[14] There are no space suits in 'Pawley's Peepholes' but the illustrations sexualize the subject, showing a shocked scantily clad woman on her bed recoiling from a male head on the floor and a near-naked woman appearing to the narrator in the street scene described above.

'Pawley's Peepholes' depicts an experimental future technology for viewing scenes from our present which has become the past. 'Opposite Number' (originally 'Opposite Numbers', 1954) stays with scientific experimentation, this time to reify time by creating images of characters at different moments, in this case the narrator who confronts a duplicate of himself to his dismay. 'Pillar to Post' (1951) also challenges the presumption of identity being singular when an amputee experiences what might have been an extended drug-induced hallucination. Right from the beginning, the story problematizes identity by presenting a letter from a law firm describing the case of a client with one name claiming to be an heir with a completely different name. These legal documents frame the main body of the narrative, which is a 'statement' by the individual in question. The latter simultaneously experiences a hallucination of waking in an alternative world and at the same time analyses his experiences, initially drawing contrasts with De Quincey's *Confessions of an English Opium-Eater* and Coleridge's 'Kubla Khan'. These bolster the actuality of the alternate world where a scientist has been experimenting in the transference of identity from one body to another.

'Dumb Martian' (1952) parodies colonialism by transposing it to Mars, where an astronaut buys a young Martian woman (a 'Mart', as he calls her) and attempts to convert her into a simulation of an Earth woman. Lellie is used by him to counter the massive expanses of time and space which hit home when he lands on a small trading planet. The brief presence of a geologist questions Duncan's presumption that Lellie is simply stupid and dumb in the literal sense of being unable to speak. As Lellie becomes aware of her exploitation, she reverses the role of Duncan by shutting him out of the space station, sealing his fate and taking over the narrative perspective as she finally sizes up her financial assets. Reversal is also central to 'Compassion Circuit' (1954), whose title suggests a hybrid combination of feeling and technology. In a future society where robotics has become the norm, Janet finally agrees to take one for her household, an example of the 'housemaid model' with a 'black silk dress and a frilly white apron and a cap' (202). When the battery-run 'maid' is in place, 'she' engages in dialogues with Janet, stressing the poor design of humans. Weakened by an undisclosed illness, Janet has to be taken to hospital, where her husband discovers to his horror that she has changed into a robot. In his foreword Wyndham describes this tale as a 'neo-Gothick trifle', but it is one carrying a satirical view of a housewife's domestic tasks as a kind of automatism.

Wyndham opens his foreword to *The Seeds of Time* with the following definition of a science-fiction story which he quotes with unqualified approval as 'one which presupposes a technology, or an effect of technology, or a disturbance in the natural order, such as humanity, up to the time of writing, has not in actual fact experienced'.[15] This definition appeared in Edmund Crispin's introduction to *Best SF: Science Fiction Stories* which he edited for Faber in 1955. Crispin was the pen name of Bruce Montgomery (1921–1978), author of detective novels and film scores, who published seven *Best SF* collections between 1955 and 1970, all with a mainstream publisher.[16] In this way Crispin helped to establish the standing of science fiction in Britain and rescue it from neglect'.[17] Wyndham would have particularly appreciated the fact that in his explanation of SF Crispin played down the element of prophecy and the importance of science, distinguishing it from the more sensational 'space-opera' and stressing that it was a genre which appealed to the intellect. On a more personal level, Wyndham must have been gratified that the first *Best SF* included 'Dumb Martian' in its contents and 'Una' in *Best SF 2*.[18]

In 1951 Wyndham contributed a 'novelette' called 'The Red Stuff', set in the year 2051, to *Marvel Science Stories*, then experiencing a brief revival. The magazine included stories by Jack Williamson and that same year a feature on Dianetics by L. Ron Hubbard. In August 1951 a special feature ran under the title 'Where will the first spaceship go?' with contributions from the American author Judith Merril, whose atomic war novel *Shadow on the Hearth* had appeared in 1950, and the German-American rocket scientist Willy Ley. In most of the *Marvel* stories, interplanetary travel is an established fact, a fact emphasized in the opening of Wyndham's narrative, which presents a government warning that a lunar station must stay closed for the foreseeable future. Apart from stimulating the reader's curiosity to learn the reason for this measure, Wyndham evokes an institutionalized network of space stations extending to the Moon, Mars and beyond.

The facility to be closed is the Clarke Lunar Station, almost certainly named after Arthur C. Clarke, who by the time of writing had become a long-standing friend of Wyndham's. In 'The Red Stuff' the name is commented on explicitly as deriving from the 'octogenarian Doctor of Physics who did so much to further space-travel'.[19] Clarke had recently, in 1948, graduated from King's College London with a degree in physics and maths. From the same period he had begun publishing books on space travel – *Interplanetary Flight* (1950) and *The Exploration of Space* (1951). His fiction was beginning to appear in the same magazines as Wyndham's and his 1951 novel *The Sands of Mars* included a facility called 'Space Station One' which 'had been Man's first stepping-stone to the stars'.[20]

79

In 'The Red Stuff' Clarke features as a formative figure in the practice of space travel, but his status is offset by the central mystery of the narrative indicated through its title. 'Stuff' is a deliberately non-scientific term for a mysterious substance. Whereas Clarke repeatedly shows characters applying science to cope with difficulties and dangers in space, Wyndham presents a sequence of professional reports which all fail to explain the phenomena under investigation. Initially we are told of a spaceship – *Madge G.* – picking up signs of a steel 'message globe' near one of the moons of Jupiter. As radio contact is established, Wyndham detaches the perspective from the spaceship in order to stress the enigmatic nature of the object:

> Nearly a thousand miles away in space the 21/2-foot-diameter steel globe revolved slowly as it drifted in a leisurely way upon the orbit into which it had fallen. To all appearance it was as inert as any other fragment of flotsam in the void. Then gradually, almost imperceptibly at first, its revolution began to slow. (41)

'Steel' implies that the object is man-made, but could it be a piece of industrial waste? Having an orbit means that its motion is not random, but again the change implies some kind of response to the radio signals from the spaceship. Delicately and gradually the sphere is manoeuvred close to the vessel until it attaches magnetically, clinging 'like a limpet', and there the first episode concludes.

The second chapter presents the contents of the mysterious message globe, particular emphasis going to a red asteroid, apparently glowing with a colour 'red as blood'. On contact with the spaceship it spreads over the instruments and masks the windows. Passing analogies imply that the substance is somehow organic, but essentially it remains an enigma – as it does throughout the narrative. The third episode consists mainly of a dialogue between two spaceships, a service vessel called *Annabelle* and *Circe* from Space Control. Once again the red substance is examined but dismissed as 'muck', 'mucous' or a 'blob'. And still there are hints of its vitality as it apparently makes contact with one vessel:

> The stuff had gathered in a kind of mound beneath the *Circe*, and flung out towards her a vast shapeless limb of itself, a reaching pseudopod like a licking red tongue. (59)

Wyndham hints at the monstrous in such lines, suggesting a conscious organism with a life of its own, but at the same time has one of the speakers ask himself 'what is life?' The immediate effect is of a displaced expansive amoeba somehow embodying an impulse, but the threat of an unknown predatory organism appears to be contained when the pilots discover its vulnerability to fire, which saves *Circe* from being swamped. However, the coda to the narrative revives the threat when it is recorded that specimen bottles of the red substance have been leaking and might contaminate the surface of the Moon.

From the same year as 'The Red Stuff' Wyndham reverses the usual pattern of space-age fiction in 'And the Walls Came Tumbling Down...' (1951), which takes its title from a nineteenth-century spiritual 'Joshua Fought the Battle of Jericho'. Here the sheer power of the voices of the Israelites causes the walls of a city closed to them to collapse. Like 'The Red Stuff', Wyndham's story opens as a report narrative, outlining in note form the problematic result of an 'expedition' against unknown aliens on another planet, but without specifics. It comes, therefore, as a shock when a commander records that 'this planet, Earth, is one hell of a spot'.[21] Instead of an Earth-focused perspective, we have that of an extraterrestrial being who can articulate his expedition to our planet in clear language and who therefore cannot simply be dismissed as alien. On the contrary, first our planet and then human beings are described in a clinical scientific language, which ironically questions our assumptions of superiority. Earth is described as a 'disgusting and dangerous dump with the potentialities of paradise' (68). It is waterlogged and – even more important – its inhabitants have a defence system capable of destroying the incoming spaceships. It gradually emerges that the newcomers are silicon-based beings in search of the raw materials they need for survival. In *Startling Stories*, where the story originally appeared, it carried a header declaring 'A Silicon Being Reports on Our Planet!' which loses the satirical effect of us being lulled into the false security of assuming a domestic attempt at exploration before realizing that the Earthlings are actually being presented as alien. Once they land at an appropriate point for prospecting for silicon and construct a 'redoubt', the newcomers encounter their first humans, who initially are scarcely distinguished from their vehicles. Then the latter are subjected to behaviourist analysis, with the conclusion being drawn that Earthlings have an instinctive tendency to hostility 'projected from an orifice a little below the lenses' (78).

The premise of much interplanetary fiction is that conflict between species is inevitable, or at least that seems to be the impulse guiding responses from Earth to the newcomers. However, the latter's approach is detached and scientific, where the physical signs of human response are given priority over any kind of inner or subjective life. Here and throughout the story the language estranges us from human norms and forces an external perspective on the reader, inviting us to reassess presumptions about human superiority. The newcomers attempt communication, but without success, hence the conclusion that 'they are obtuse coarse hopeless clods as insensitive to thought as they are to sound' (86). Wyndham never specifies too closely what form or substance determines the newcomers. References to silicon could be a trope of fragility in that sound waves from the Earthlings literally shake the newcomers to pieces, and the story concludes with one narrator undergoing the agony of death. The title within its biblical context would imply a triumph of piety over adversity, but here rather suggests the failure of rationality and difference with no triumphal implications.

Although the 1954 story collection *Jizzle* is often listed as science fiction, the stories have more in common with fantasy. Mostly drawn from the years 1949 to 1954, they had originally appeared in such publications as *Collier's* in the USA, the fiction magazine *Argosy*, the tabloid *Everybody's Weekly* and even *Woman's Journal*, all suggesting that Wyndham in this period was making a conscious effort to diversify his publications.

The title story (from *Collier's* 1949) sets a keynote in focusing on a performing chimp, bought as a commercial speculation by the owner of a sideshow promoting a 'Psychological Stimulator'. The monkey can draw pictures of human subjects and shocks its owner into a fit of jealousy by depicting his wife with another man. The narrative deflects possible scepticism over the monkey's supposed skill by suggesting the owner's acceptance of it, and the tale, like many others, ends with the cryptic coda of another picture, this time of the owner.[22] Theatre also informs 'Esmeralda' (1952), which describes an American performing flea, according to the narrator 'far and away the best performer

I ever had in my show'.[23] Esmeralda is used as a means of dramatizing the rival attractions of an assistant called Molly and another performer called Helga. The former 'could tell an artist when she saw one' (63), which means in practice seeing through the latter, who drops out of the act. 'More Spinned Against' (1953)[24] continues the use of other species, this time drawing on the myth of Arachne to depict the experiences of a woman married to a collector of spiders. She engages in a comic dialogue with a giant spider and swaps roles with it, only to find that she may be killed and consumed as a result.

The use of other species in these stories satirically reflects on the situations of their human characters, and in a similar spirit Wyndham sometimes depicts the commercialization of subjects like the ageing process. 'Technical Slip' (1949), for instance, opens with a character who is dying but who is offered a life extension as a business deal, offered on the basis that capital has replaced moral well-being. When he visits his old home, to his astonishment he finds himself being treated as if he were 50 years younger. Thus the desire to extend his lifespan has resulted in a return to his childhood, complicated by the fact that he can alter the past. Where this story pivots on a disorienting reversion, 'How Do I Do?' (1953) evokes a young woman confronted with numerous guidance leaflets about the future. Consulting a fortune-teller, she undergoes a crisis where she finds herself in the future with a husband. That is disturbing enough, but worse still is the difference from her future self, which is explained by a companion as follows: 'you just *seem* to yourself to go on being the same person. But [...] as the cells that make you are always gradually being replaced, you can't really be *all* the same person' (85). Frances's attempts to discover the future backfire into a challenge to the self's stable singularity.

Gender plays an important role in some these stories, especially in 'Perforce to Dream' (1953), which takes its title from Hamlet's famous reflections on the 'sleep of death'. Here two women have just published near-identical novels which draw on their dreams of 'idyllic romance' which compensate for the tedium of their daily lives. They then attend a theatrical performance where the two roles of leading lady and authoress are played by the same woman. The true climax comes when the female audience turns on a male psychologist who falls to his death from a box. The tale closes with these final lines: 'And who shall say how many tears flowed upon how many pillows for the dream that did not come that night, nor never again ...?' (164). Wyndham blurs the differences between fantasy, fiction and theatre, suggesting a continuity between all three no doubt helped by the story's original appearance in the magazine *Woman's Journal*. The gendering of fantasy is also central to 'Reservation Deferred', which focuses on a dying a teenage girl. Amanda's thoughts have turned inevitably to her own demise, but she is unable to glean any information about heaven from a cleric or her mother. Next she is visited by a ghost called Virginia who – far from terrifying her – serves as a companion who describes the Oriental and Nordic sections of the afterlife, delivering the final ironic message that 'they're all men's heavens, and that's hell for a woman' (169).

The stories in *Jizzle* frequently shift in time and place, one of the most dramatic being 'Confidence Trick' (from *Fantastic*, 1953), which opens in a rush-hour scene on the London Underground. The focal character is vowing to himself 'never again' as a newcomer to the situation unfamiliar with the estranging effects of the journey. At one point his train stops in total darkness and the lights go out momentarily, all quite plausible on the deep-level line from Bank station. When the train starts up again, he attempts to pull the emergency handle, but with no effect. It seems as if the train is heading for some kind of Hell. Finally it stops at the 'end of the line', which metaphorically could suggest the imminent deaths of the passengers, but here again Wyndham plays with effects. The 'demons' at the station are trying to sell products to the hapless passengers and in an apparent return to normality, reports filter through of an accident on the underground. Cut to a group of passengers outside the station and one pushes a young man to his death under a bus, claiming that he was planning to attack the bank. The reader is left with unresolved questions about the narrative: was the hell-journey a collective hallucination? Was the main danger in the journey the other passengers? We are never told.

The story which engages in the most explicit dialogue with science fiction had been extensively revised, extended and retitled since its 1937 publication as 'A Perfect Creature'. 'Una' is narrated by an official in an organization similar to the RSPCA

CONSIDER HER WAYS AND OTHER STORIES

visiting a country village where strange creatures have been sighted which resemble upright turtles, or could it have been a hoax? One witness, another official named Alfred, is convinced that they have been created by a 'super-vivisectionist', but that may be because he has read Wells's *Island of Doctor Moreau*, which is explicitly referenced early in the story. The narrator's party visits Dr Dixon, a local scientist who makes no attempt to conceal the fact that he has been experimentally constructing humanoids and who shows his visitors his latest construction, which is cone-shaped, lacking a head, with three legs. In the original story he is simply named 'Number One' as if starting a series, but in *Jizzle* the humanoid is gendered, carrying the same name as the fair maiden in Spenser's *Faerie Queen*. As soon as 'she' sees the visitors she starts to bellow 'I want Alfred!' and here the story in effect shifts genre into slapstick. Breaking free from her cell, she pursues Alfred through the village, eventually falling to 'her' death in the river. In a sense Dixon could be taken as another Moreau, ultimately unable to control his creations. But the climax reads like a grotesque parody of female sexual attraction threatening nobody (except Alfred) until the creature falls to its death.

The title novella of *Consider Her Ways* (1961), first published in 1956, is a more sustained fantasia on gender with a female narrator, unusual in Wyndham, although its austere opening impresses by giving us virtually no information at all:

> I hung in a timeless, spaceless, forceless void that was neither light, nor dark. I had entity, but no form; awareness, but no senses; mind, but no memory. I wondered, is this – this nothingness – my soul? And it seemed that I had wondered that always, and should go on wondering it for ever. (1)[25]

There is no setting, nothing but an unlocated voice which is surprisingly articulate about its own state. This absence of information is shortly relieved and naturalized as the speaker apparently regains consciousness in some kind of hospital. Addressed as 'Mother', she begins to register her surroundings, but retains a suspicion that she is living out a dream or hallucination and that all her visual experiences are 'chockful of symbolic content'. Although she registers a background uncertainty about what is happening to her, the descriptive data we are given is precise and detailed. As she is driven along a road she notes that all the buildings along the way are uniformly neat and clean, and that the only traffic appears to be commercial. When she arrives 'home', she is named as Mother Orchis and experiences a major shock when she confronts her image in a mirror: 'In front of me stood an outrageous travesty: an elephantine female form, looking the more huge for its pink swathings' (13–14). The last term suggests a displacement of swaddling clothes off a new-born baby onto the adult, and more disturbingly evokes a complete dissociation of body from consciousness.

In fact, dissociation is the dominant effect of the novella's opening sections as the narrator realizes that all her norms are being questioned. Although she is told that she has just produced four babies, she has no memory of their birth. When she asks for something to read, the response is shock and horror, especially when she shows that she can write. This effect is even signalled in Wyndham's title, which alters the gender (and species) of the passage in *Proverbs* 6.vi which reads 'Go to the ant, thou sluggard; consider its ways and be wise'. Ants are a species used repeatedly by Wyndham to question our presumptions about human norms, but his new title has foregrounded the female as if a separate species, and this is reflected in the most striking characteristic of the world that the narrator confronts: there are no men and the social roles of the women are reflected in their physical stature. Thus Mothers, i.e. breeders, are enormous, the Servitors are very short, and the Workers (or 'Amazons', as the narrator calls them) have short hair and biceps 'like a man's'. The only figure to fit the narrator's (and reader's) implicit norm is the doctor she meets. Although ostensibly a doctor, her role is more that of an enforcer, where any 'abnormal' behaviour by the narrator is interpreted as pathological.

As the narrator regains her memory, she remembers her name as Jane, the fact that she had followed medical training, and also that the love of her life had died in an accident. Eventually she is handed over to an elderly historian called Laura, where who supplies the story linking Jane's present to the future that she finds herself in. It is she who outlines the eugenic utopia that she is encountering, one based on the principle that a woman is the 'vessel of life' and that man is only there to enable reproduction. The future regime is run on the Darwinian line that the main impetus in life is the 'will to power' and that, modelling its methods on those of the ants, an anonymous Directorate has reorganized society on functional lines. Every objection from Jane is dismissed as her 'conditioning' and the historian ridicules her conservatism in clinging to myths promoted by the male authorities of the past that 'women must never for a moment be allowed to forget their sex, and compete as equals' (44), and that romance served as a justification for male prerogatives in promoting the myth that 'it was sex, civilized into romantic love, that made the world go round' (49). The historian glosses over the issue of reproduction but does explain the demise of men as the result of an experimental drug mutating which was designed to exterminate predatory rats. Amy Binns has argued that the novella should be read as Wyndham's 'continuing attempt to work out his own beliefs as to whether the sexes could live together without the stronger preying on the weaker'.[26]

By this point in the narrative Jane has regained her memory and has been instructed in the rationale of the future society she is visiting. Since she is clearly a misfit there, she agrees with the authorities that she should return to her original present, but the only means to achieve that seems to be to repeat the original experiment when she performed the role of guinea pig in testing an experimental drug. Jane repeatedly expresses uncertainty about the status of her own narrative, whether it is a dream, hallucination, or a 'kind of pre-vision of an inevitable, predestined future' (64). If the latter is the case, she is unable to change anything. Alternatively, she might be able to play destiny and accordingly her account is framed as a written document which she determines to use against Perrigan, to justify her action in hunting him down and shooting him. The coda to the novella consists of a dialogue between a solicitor and one of the doctors Jane has been working with. Ostensibly their discussion focuses on her guilt or innocence, but it also has a metafictional dimension in that both men have 'received' the narrative and are thus in the position of readers assessing its narrative plausibility.

'Consider Her Ways' combines a dystopian future with a narrative of time displacement, and other stories in this collection further reflect Wyndham's interest in disruptions to time sequences. In 'Odd', set in the year 1958, a young man encounters a London businessman who is convinced he is living in 1906. During their discussion the latter registers a sense that he must be having 'some silly kind of dream' (75), which he attempts to rationalize by having been struck by a tram, although they hadn't run in that street for years. After his death records emerge of his accident, which thus cannot be dismissed as fantasy.

'Stitch in Time' (1961) fleshes out an opening domestic situation where the elderly Mrs Dolderson is enjoying the 'timeless' comforts of her home and garden. It is quietly indicated that her illusion of avoiding change has been undermined by modifications to her house and by her perception that thanks to her age she has begun to feel like a 'stranger in another people's world' (112). After dozing off, she wakes to see her lover from the past apparently reincarnated before her. Wyndham frequently includes a commentator, and Mrs Dolderson performs this role. Accordingly, it is Arthur, the young man from 1913, who needs reassurance when jets roar by overhead (the story's present is 1963) and whose appearance and behaviour trigger a memory of her son Harold 'talking about dimensions, of shifting the into different planes, speaking of time as though it were simply another dimension' (119–120). Wyndham is careful not to credit her with too much awareness, although her dialogue with her former lover is a model of patient tact in gradually revealing his new location in time. In common with the other stories about time, this narrative has two transition points, one where Mrs Dolderson falls asleep and one where she apparently wakes in her room to see her son standing by her. He explains that she had evidently fainted and that the young man with her needed treatment, thereby confirming that the reappearance of Arthur wasn't just a fantasy of hers. The son Harold sets up his machine again for Arthur's return and he disappears.

By now the pattern for these time narratives should be emerging. Wyndham sets up a realistically detailed scene, then introduces the time warp through a transitioning episode. The perspective character experiences or witnesses an incongruous experience, which is explained in so far as the 'visitor' character and their circumstances authenticate a time shift. If a machine like Harold's is used, it is never described. The stories' emphasis falls entirely on the dichotomy of time, and the commentary provided in each case serves to exclude interpretations of these

CONSIDER HER WAYS AND OTHER STORIES

disparities as merely fantasies, dreams or sublimation. Typically, the stories conclude with details which prevent closure and which leave the us uncertain about the implications of what we have just read.

From the same collection, 'Random Quest' is one of the more complex of these stories in opening with a meeting between a doctor – the perspective character – and a young man named Trafford who is hunting for an obscure member of the doctor's family, named Ottilie. The latter starts his conversation with the visitor by telling the story of Trafford's search to Trafford himself, as if a third person. As his account proceeds the doctor diagnoses no pathological symptoms in the other, only an element of fear. And then Trafford takes over the narration, opening it with the chance accident of a bus crashing into a shop front. The story is set in the 1950s and, possibly triggered by the accident, Trafford then finds more and more incongruities in the London scenes before him – the widespread use by women of ankle-length dresses, the intact church which had been badly damaged in the war, and other cases. Trafford meets a friend from before the war, who reads his behaviour as strange in the extreme, and then Trafford experiences a 'fracturing' of himself when he goes to his former apartment, meets his girlfriend, and even encounters his younger self. His initial dislocation is mainly spatial, 'as if one had been dropped abruptly into a foreign city' (148), now becomes more disturbing:

> Her [Ottolie's] Colin Trafford looked like me [...] indeed, up to a point, that point somewhere in 1926–7, he *was* me. We had, I gathered, some mannerisms in common and voices that were similar [then he notes] the scar on the left side of the forehead which was exclusively his, yet, in a sense, I was him and he was me. (156–157)

The pronoun shifts in this passage reflect Trafford's uneasy shifts between identity and difference. It is as if he has gone back to the pre-war period and met a version of himself which develops autonomously as he makes a career as a novelist. 'Stitch in Time' follows a Wellsian strategy of glancing at other dimensions, but now Trafford speculates on the meaning of 'moment' as dependent on multiple observers, as if he has somehow changed perceptual role, but this is brief and tentative.

The story ends inconclusively with the suggestion that Ottolie may have married the doctor, which awkwardly straddles the drama of identity and the romantic relations of both main characters.

Apart from the stories in the collection dealing with time breaks, 'Oh, Where, Now, is Peggy MacRafferty?' satirizes the Hollywood publicity machine. It focuses on a knowledgeable but naïve Irish girl who wants to make a career for herself in the movies. After her first breakthrough on winning a talent competition, she undergoes a series of transformations whereby she is given a new name, instructed on how to develop her body, given speech training – hence a pointed allusion to Henry Higgins of *Pygmalion* and *My Fair Lady* fame – and groomed to become one of the many 'Lolos' in the business, by which is meant the stereotypical actresses loosely modelled on Gina Lollobrigida. In the coda to the story, when her talent scout attempts to meet her on returning to the USA, it proves to be impossible because the plane contains 'Thirty-six made-to-measure Lolos' (109). It is as if Peggy has vanished in the Hollywood machine.

This story is basically a satirical parable on the film business, and further evidence of Wyndham's desire to open up the range of subjects and methods in his postwar stories. Throughout this chapter we have seen how the narrative means regularly become part of the stories' subjects, which range from satire to comedy, often with reversals of perspective. The last story to be published in Wyndham's lifetime, 'A Life Postponed' (1968), opens with the abrupt and arresting declaration that 'love is a guerrilla'.[27] In one sense this begins a love story, but the two lovers, Cyra and Willie, each meditate on the concept of love rather than their persons, producing a 'conflict between love and principles' (119). Willie wonders about the working of the Life Force, offset by a gloomy sense of the world heading for disaster.[28] Unable to resist Cyra's desire for marriage, Willie leaves, at which point she discovers that he has secretly joined an experimental biological research unit and been frozen into suspended animation until 2095. The story then shifts to Willie's perspective as he slowly regains consciousness in the future. He scarcely has time to register a perception that the future is not as bad as he expected before he is joined by Cyra. No explanation is given of how she tracked him down and the story concludes with the two agreeing to marry and have babies. The story revolves around gender, implying Cyra is the more enterprising of the two, and around time; despite being preoccupied with the future, Willie holds a job in a London museum. The story is typical of Wyndham's postwar writings too in using its narrative appeals to the reader's speculative responses, reflecting Wyndham's evolving conception of science fiction, to which we now turn.

5

Wyndham on SF

From 1937 right up to his death in 1969, Wyndham was a regular reviewer of science fiction and commentator on the development of that genre. This writing offers an evolving context for his own fiction and shows how he was constantly revising his conception of SF, measured at every point by bearings from the fiction of H. G. Wells. He read *The Time Machine* around the age of 12, his first known venture into fiction was a pastiche piece connected with *The Island of Doctor Moreau*, and throughout his career Wyndham's fiction was punctuated with allusions to Wells's writings.

Wyndham's first step towards critical writing on SF was his successful entry for the banner slogan competition in 1930 for the magazine *Air Wonder Stories*, which he won with 'Future Flying Fiction'. However, his major step was to start contributing to *Scientifiction: The British Fantasy Review*, a fanzine founded in 1937 and edited by Walter H. Gillings. Its title applied the term coined in 1916 by the writer Hugo Gernsback, whose novel *Ralph 124C 41+* had been serialized in the magazine *Modern Electronics* in 1911. Gillings's agenda was to distinguish a British SF readership from their American counterparts, hence the inaugural issue proclaimed: 'the Era of Science Fiction in England has begun!' and highlighted the American preference for gadgetry and sensational violent action centring on a male hero. Thus one article listed what was not going to appear in British SF, namely 'rocket-ships, thought-machines, robots, force beams, disintegrator rays and other mechanical marvels [...] depicted on Mars, Venus, Mercury and other remote planets'.[1] It was therefore consistent for the journal to promote emerging British writers like Eric Frank Russell, who had only recently secured acceptance of his stories after being rejected by several

American magazines. In interview Russell stressed his determination to depict 'ordinary human beings [...] and not up-to-date versions of Marzipan the Magician'. Turning his back on transatlantic gadgetry, he insisted that the golden rule of SF was to 'make it plausible'.[2]

The inaugural issue of *Scientifiction* also carried an interview with Wyndham after noting the successful serializations of *The Secret People* in 1935 and *Stowaway to Mars* in 1936, the latter published in book form that same year with the title *Planet Plane*. In the interview Wyndham modestly underplayed his successes as luck, and Gillings set the keynote of Wyndham's attitude to SF when he recorded: 'he does not believe in sacrificing literary quality for sensational new ideas and hustling action'.[3] He also noted that, despite his growing interest in SF, Wyndham was continuing to write detective fiction.

Wyndham's first contributions to *Scientifiction* followed its editorial line in contrasting American with European practice. He opened his review of Karel Capek's *War with the Newts* (1936) by declaring: 'if you want high-speed thrills, you must look elsewhere; but if you delight in the display of a vivid, yet controlled imagination, a fine sense of story-telling and a breadth of understanding, then turn to Capek whose techniques in handling the theme of race suicide stand comparison with Olaf Stapledon'.[4] Later that same year Wyndham reviewed the latter's *Star Maker*, which he praised for its 'continuous display of imaginative gymnastics' and for Stapledon's appropriation of the whole cosmos for his scenarios.[5] In a piece of polemic titled 'Why This Cosmic Wild West Stuff?', Wyndham called for a strengthening of the British tradition of SF: 'I think it is necessary to retrace and recapture some of that earlier simplicity and convincing quality, which seems to have disappeared from the American product'. In contrast with a tradition of magazine fiction, he cites a line of novelists from Wells to Stapledon and Aldous Huxley, concluding that 'the English reader prefers a different style and approach to the American. He wants better explanations, which he can believe, and he can't be spoofed quite so easily'.[6] Wyndham's subsequent critical writing was to flesh out this position but to leave its central tenets unchanged.

We should not assume that Wyndham was simply applying a nationalistic viewpoint here because, when turning his attention to the techniques used by the American Stanley G. Weinbaum, without hesitation he praised the latter's simplicity, his 'instinctive appreciation of what might be taken for granted and what must be explained', and 'equally remarkable is the restraint with which he has confined himself to a purely objective view', even when describing a scene from the twenty-third century.[7] When he reviewed a later collection of Weinbaum's stories, Wyndham placed him in contrast to the evolution of the second phase to American SF which produced 'shoddy hack-junk'. In Weinbaum, 'there was a feeling of sympathy, an enjoyment of his own invention and a gift of reticence. It was this last ability to suggest and imply while refusing elaborate explanations' which marked his genius. Sadly, Wyndham finds a deterioration in Weinbaum's later stories, where the ideas drop out and 'corny stand-bys' are substituted.[8]

As he picked up the threads of this writing from 1947 onwards, Wyndham regularly continued to review fiction of quite diverse genres for the *Fantasy Review*, again edited by Walter Gillings, who explained his policy in the opening number as follows: 'the intention is to present a selection of science fiction which [...] will appeal irresistibly to the greatly enlarged circle of British fantasy followers'.[9] In addition to a regular reviews section, the journal also carried feature articles like a forum addressing the question 'Can Science Fiction Prophesy?' with contributions from John W. Campbell, Groff Conklin and an interview with Arthur C. Clarke.

Wyndham's interests extended beyond science fiction, however. His first contribution to the *Fantasy Review* was a review in 1947 of William Hope Hodgson's *The House on the Borderland*, which balanced a recognition of the latter's status against some criticism of his methods. Stressing the period of Hodgson's stories (1907–1912), Wyndham pays tribute to the latter's status as a formative figure in weird fiction and praises his 'superb ability to hint and suggest', to show the 'half-seen, half-comprehended', which greatly outweighs eccentricities like his use of 'pseudo-archaic language'.[10] Wyndham's respect for Hodgson's narrative skills did not extend to the writer Frank Baker, whose novel *Before I Go Hence* describes the contacts between the tenant of a deserted house and the spirit of a deceased Anglican priest. For Wyndham this work had a poor structure and described implausible influences; hence the title of the review – 'Did Mr. Baker Lose His Way?' ironically echoes that of Baker's 1945 novel *Mr. Allenby Loses the Way*. At several points Wyndham implies that the Gothic has run its course, a perspective he makes quite explicit in his review of Arthur Machen's stories, the more recent of which he finds lacking the 'wonder, uneasiness and terror' associated with the genre. Wyndham evokes a writer with a problematic relation to the taste of his time, and thus concludes that 'much in Machen's stories suggests to me an uncertain man, ill at ease in the world in which he must live'.[11]

Again in contrast, when Wyndham turns to a collection of short stories by Gerald Heard, the friend and collaborator of Aldous Huxley, he contrasts conception with execution, declaring: 'Here is versatility of interest backed by wide knowledge, careful consideration and accomplished writing to hold the attention'.[12] The title story 'The Great Fog', may have played a part in the genesis of *The Day of the Triffids* which he was working on in the late 1940s in its account of a major disruption to the order of nature. Like Wyndham, Heard opens his narrative with a cryptic understatement: 'The first symptom was a mildew'.[13] A mysterious mould attaches itself to trees and spreads round the world from its origins in eastern Europe, generating local fog fields which expand and merge. In short, the whole balance of nature becomes disrupted. Again like Wyndham, at every stage in their development these symptoms are subjected to scrutiny and analysis until the lead scientist declares in a public address that 'the balance of life has been upset'.[14] There is no resolution to the action, only speculation that the Creator has presented humanity with a challenge. In that respect, the story resembles a parable on human knowledge, exploiting the traditional associations of fog with incomprehension.

When he reviewed works closer to SF, Wyndham remained cautious and judicious in his judgements. Despite his continuing respect for Olaf Stapledon's *Last and First Men* (1930) and *Star Maker* (1937), noted above, he had some reservations about *The Flames: A Fantasy* (1947), which he contrasted with the last works of Wells and which for him offered a 'simple restatement of the view that homo still shows little prospect of becoming sapiens'. Noting Stapledon's use of the traditional symbolism of sentient flames, Wyndham draws the following contrast with Wells:

> Their main dissimilarity lies in scale of view. The spirituality with which Wells was concerned was limited and almost measurable. It implies in his works that he considered man, with no great modifications, to be evolution's last word; failure, therefore, must mean utter defeat – the end. For Dr. Stapledon, however, spirit – life in evolution – is more important than such temporary manifestations of it as mankind. Were it not for that, he too might be oppressed to the same unhappy sense of futility at the prospect of the unregenerate homo astutus blundering closer to the end of his tether.[15]

The contrast is clear, though Wyndham never quite charges Stapledon with an abstract spirituality remote from the practicalities of human life. And surely there is a gesture of respect in Wyndham's concluding allusion to Wells's last book, *Mind at the End of Its Tether* (1945).

When reviewing a lighter work of SF, Wyndham raised his tone correspondingly. Covering Garnett Radcliffe's *The Lady from Venus* in 1947, which describes an attempt to take eggs from Earth back to Venus, Wyndham comments that 'numerous interplanetary ingredients, both new and familiar, are taken straight from the garden, dashed with friendly satire, dressed (undressed) with Thorne Smith, and served up in an Anita Loos bowl'.[16] Despite the suggestions of the novel having been seasoned by two American humorists, Wyndham does not ridicule the use of SF for satire and also implicitly applauds Radcliffe for not taking his narrative 'gadgets' too seriously. In a similar spirit Wyndham praised Ward Moore's *Greener Than You Think* for its satirical portrayal of an experiment gone drastically wrong. The invention of a device in California called the 'Metamorphizer' which 'will change the basic structure of any plant inoculated with it' goes so wrong that Bermuda grass grows out of control right round the world, another narrative which could have helped Wyndham devise his triffids. He praised the novel's 'combination of thriller and satire' and stated of its salesman narrator that 'Albert himself is not simply the unintelligent instrument of fate; he is the opportunist, the man who ravages the forests without planting, the farmer who rapes the land and leaves it a dustbowl'.[17]

The treatment here is convincing, whereas Wyndham levels trenchant criticism against *The Big Eye* (1949) by the American journalist and script writer Max Ehrlich. The Big Eye of the title refers to a huge reflector telescope which identifies a planet apparently heading for a collision with Earth which is predicted to happen at Christmas 1962 (the novel's present is 1960). Wyndham takes the scenario as opportunity to reflect on SF narratives, stating:

> In general, science fiction, whether intellectual, exciting or merely ropey, is most easily handled as an adventure story or a thriller; it is usually an action story where the conflict is between the protagonists and the circumstances. In the novel proper, however, conflict is the outcome of human character. It follows, therefore, that in a s-f novel there must be two conflicts running simultaneously and interlocking, and even the most expect hands have found this difficult.[18]

When the object is first spotted, the fear is that it might be a Russian missile, but it is the shift in perception to that of a planet is what provokes Wyndham's sarcasm: 'Whereas under the threat of atomic bombing this New York is all panic and flight, under that of planetary obliteration it whoops it up'.[19] The depiction of public psychology, in short, is too sweeping and inconsistent.

On the eve of the Second World War Wyndham had already begun to move his critical writings away from reviews of individual works to address broader issues. In the Summer 1939 issue of *Tales of Wonder* he contributed a piece called 'Sowing New Thoughts' where he saw SF as helping the cause of enlightened reason. 'It can', he declares, 'and one hopes that it will, become part of the defence against the rising tide of superstition and Dark Ages beliefs'. He continues:

> Behind the greatest scientific romances there is a purpose [...] they are sowing new thoughts in the reader's mind; the products which go to build an individual's convictions, and his only defence against being fair game for any meretricious, nonsensical or deliberately retrograde doctrine which may be fed to him.[20]

Wyndham used his 1948 review of Weinbaum's *The Black Flame* to reflect on the history of the SF genre, which he explained initially as an intensification of all effects:

Bigger is better, and faster is better. For proper thrill and excitement, therefore, wars must be intergalactic, with thousands of ships mounting hundreds of rays; speed must be reckoned in light-years per second, worlds be propelled from one system to another. And what about the sex angle? Hey, bring on the dancing girls!

In the ensuing orgy whole universes were vaporized, non-interacting super-men slugged their way around space more like supermaniacs. Impermeably space-suited heroes cavorted through the cosmos with curvaceous cuties inevitably clad in bathing suits – and all interest departed from the stories.[21]

Apart from its force as a piece of cultural criticism, passages like this were written at a time when Wyndham was re-inventing his own style, and they give us a direct indication of the excesses he was determined to avoid in his own fiction. The implicit direction in which he was moving was towards the avoidance of spectacle and sensation, towards localized dramas and protagonists (of both genders) defined by their thoughtfulness rather than violent action.

Under the title 'Why Blame Wells?' in the twelfth number of the *Fantasy Review* (1948–1949), Wyndham took the re-issue of Wells's *The First Men in the Moon* as an opportunity to reflect on that writer's formative influence and on the development of magazine SF since that novel's original publication in 1901. Retrospectively applying the tastes of the 1940s, he looks in vain for 'zip, pep and dynamic action' in its opening and concludes that 'this means Wells doesn't apply journalistic principles' in his fiction. Instead, we are told:

Here is real science fiction. Not science black-mask, not science adventure story (though it does not lack adventure), not science Munchausen, nor science haywire, nor science confession, but solid, basic, science fiction. Instead of a montage of this, that or the other careful slant, there is just a story, full of invention, yet so subtly smoothed that much of the thought which has gone into it appears only on examination.[22]

Wyndham attacks the hybrid compromises of SF with popular taste, excluding it from the hard-boiled crime fiction promoted by *Black Mask* since 1920 and from the 'Science Adventures' of Baron Munchausen published in 1915 by Hugo Gernsback. He concludes with a simple assertion that 'the mind of H. G. Wells, taking a thesis and logically exploring it in the light of known facts and possibilities, influenced a whole generation'.[23] Wyndham was to return to the American influence on SF in his 1955 *New Worlds* piece (see below).

From the very beginning of his career Wyndham's critical writing demonstrates a shrewd awareness of the market conditions for SF and in 'Why Blame Wells?', he identified important social changes amounting to a kind of cultural McCarthyism which was impacting on the composition and reception of SF, declaring: 'In a world that is becoming increasingly standardised and more and more afraid of other people's ideas, the channels where one may emote with decency and safety are pretty well defined'. The result, Wyndham argues, is a conservatism where 'it is safer to confine prophecy as much as possible to the field of mechanical gadgets and leave the people as they are, dissipating any tendency to real inquiry by emotional excitement directed into the proper channels'. Diagnosing a loss of freedom of expression over the last 50 years, Wyndham presents a series of ironic warnings to potential authors and editors, citing the notorious Motion Picture Association of America, chaired by Will H. Hays, which promulgated the censorious Production Code of 1930:

> Warning signs are borrowed from the Hays Office: Religion – do not disturb – penalty 20 per cent or more subscribers; Sex – Do not inquire – penalty, parental Comstockery; Social system – beware of F.B.I.; International politics – proceed with caution – everybody touchy (and yesterday's .friend may be tomorrow's enemy, which can be awkward); Nationalism – do not ignore – penalty for foreign triumphing, large disappointment of readers; and so on, and so on.

In the face of such oppressive potential censorship, Wyndham concludes drily that 'on the whole, it is much less trouble to keep to a path which leads to a happy-ever-after in a gadgeteer's heaven'.[24]

During the 1950s Wyndham moved his critical writing further away from reviews to broader essays on SF, aimed at analysing and promoting that genre. In an article for the American magazine *Authentic Science Fiction Monthly* of February 1953, he confronted a presumption that to write a SF story 'a bright idea is enough'. Wyndham insists on the crucial importance of story, by which he includes execution, and also points out that any aspiring SF writer has to engage with a social conservatism, a 'taboo on any serious suggestion of change in social habits'. The situation with SF would seem bleak were it not for the recent emphasis on story placed by magazine editors. The result is some signs of improvement:

> There begins to be more attention to characterisation, and though imagination must place its feet very carefully to avoid stepping on the thickset prejudices, imaginative stories – real stories that are not just processions of fights and bangs – where the invention produces an effect on the people involved, are beginning to emerge.[25]

The following year Wyndham addressed a British readership in more overtly critical terms. In a guest editorial called 'The Pattern of Science Fiction' for *Science Fantasy* (another magazine edited initially by Walter Gillings) in March 1954, he again bemoans the catch-all function of the 'Science Fiction' label, which covers a variety of sins ranging from the incomprehensible to the pornographic, particularly as 'it overlays and brings into contempt a type of imaginative story which once maintained quite conscientious standards of form and writing in a niche of its own'. Is there any hope for the genre then? Wyndham falls back on his conviction that 'a tale must proceed from its premiss with adequate reason and logic', The first principle he enunciates is that 'in the imaginative story there must be a wholeness and a logic which is not cut across either by silly assumptions used simply to make a situation more exciting, or by inventions called up on the spirit of the moment just to get the characters out of a jam'. In short, the first golden rule is consistency. And then science should feature, but not in a didactic or fantastic way. If it is impossible for the reader to conceive how a device might work, then, he declares, 'I should not know whether I was contemplating a possibility or a piece of sheer hocus'. In other words, science should figure as part of a narrative 'backbone'. Despite his title, rather than a pattern, Wyndham spells out a general principle of narrative construction which is actually broader than SF because he draws analogies with detective fiction. Although he had turned away from that genre before the war, he never forgot it when identifying a methodology for SF. It is also striking that by the mid-1950s, he perceives SF to have become so institutionalized that he can praise the annual

Fantasy Awards for their attempts 'to pick out the best examples of controlled imagination – imagination working from data or theory within accepted limitations'.[26]

Breadth of reference now became central. In his 1954 article 'Roar of Rockets!' for example, Wyndham opens his comments on the SF genre within its perceived tension with detective fiction: 'The simple fact behind the arrival of science-fiction in the book world is that there has been too much murder going for too long'.[27] He had already commented on this generic rivalry in 1951 and it was to become an important theme in his subsequent criticism.[28] Once again cultural contrasts came to the fore when Wyndham acknowledged the 'much more extensive indoctrination that the Americans have received from magazines, comic-strips and television serials'. The irony is that the two genres took shape in the same period, but that the one enjoyed fresh surges of productivity while the other 'acquired the repellent label "science-fiction", which it has had to drag about like a ball-and-chain ever since'.[29] Throughout his critical writings Wyndham complained about this 'repellent label', as he called it in 1954, for being vague and carrying associations with the worst American stories on the market. Its use developed steadily through the 1950s, but only late in his career did Wyndham come to accept this label.

In making his case for SF, Wyndham guides us through its taxonomy, which he breaks down into four categories: the juvenile, the adolescent, the technician's story and the implicatory story. The first of these was dismissively characterized as a mode 'in which mentally retarded supermen play cowboys and indians all over the galaxy'; the second merely added 'starlet-type young women'; and the third was 'conscientious in its use of scientific principles'. It is the fourth category, however, which offers real possibilities of satire and other effects. Interestingly, in this section Wyndham divides his examples equally between Britain and America; between Huxley's dystopias, Orwell's *Nineteen Eighty-Four* and Katherine Burdekin's *Swastika Night* (1937) on the one hand, and Elmer Rice's *A Voyage to Puerilia* (1930), Sinclair Lewis's *It Can't Happen Here* (1935) and Kurt Vonnegut's *Player Piano* (1952) on the other. Wyndham concludes by describing a mock-serious war between the two genres. Drawing on SF imagery, he declares: 'I welcome the coming end of detective-dictatorship over such a vast proportion of light literature. Let the rockets thin them out, let the time-machines bewilder them, let the robots chase them out of their dug-in positions'.[30]

With some variations, Wyndham's classification of SF into a small number of subsets recurred throughout the 1950s and 1960s, always with one of the latter being privileged as the most promising medium of innovation. In contrast with 'veritable SF', 'pseudo-SF', and SF film, in a 1957 review this role was occupied by 'speculative fiction', whose role Wyndham dramatizes by declaring that 'after a long independent existence it was kidnapped by reviewers and booksellers, and put behind this wire'.[31] In a short 1958 essay on the 'Scientific Novel', he explained SF generically as a 'gadget-equipped adaptation of the Western and the Thriller'.[32] Lastly in a 1962 article, Wyndham again rang changes to his categories when he identified the Vernian type, space-opera, horror-SF descending from *Frankenstein*, and 'reasoned fantasy' whose great practitioner was Wells.[33]

Cultural contrasts again recur in 1955 when Wyndham edited a selection of material from John Carnell's *New Worlds* magazine, which for him had 'foiled the American inundation of the British periodical market'. In his introduction Wyndham warned of the potential threat of a 'transatlantic deluge of well-fed glossies and bulky pulps' which was difficult to counter amid the austerities of postwar Britain. Using a more nuanced contrast between detective fiction and SF, he admitted tendencies common to both genres, noting that 'just as the term "crime story" carries a connotation suggesting the "action story" filled with guns and car-chases, so the term "science fiction" carries a first connotation suggesting 'super space-ships and galactic warfare'. The terms have now shifted from a broad sweeping contrast between genres to a contrast within each genre between crude sensationalism and a more sophisticated – to use Wyndham's own term, *implicatory* – form of narrative. Thus the intelligent detective story centres on the 'posing and logical solution of a problem' and he continues with the second genre: 'now, good science fiction differs from galactic gallivanting by doing just this. It asks: "What would happen if ...?" It puts the proposition forward in story form, and then does its best to answer it'. In that respect both modes of fiction come to resemble each other and their differences prove to be 'much more apparent than real: they lie chiefly in the décor, and the wider terrain over which the game is played, and in requiring a different background knowledge from the reader'.[34] Both centre on logical deduction. The issue of *New Worlds* for May 1955 carried a profile of Wyndham, where he is summarized as feeling that there are two forms of SF story: one 'where the gadget or the technical development is all that matters' and 'the extrapolatory story in which people like us are affected by the shifting about them of the technological scenery and props'.[35]

New Worlds evolved from a pre-war fanzine called *Novae Terrae* (1936–1939), the last four numbers of which were edited by John Carnell. Its backing company failed, and Carnell made attempts throughout 1940, with 'invaluable help' from Wyndham and others to get a substitute off the ground, but without success.[36] The journal was revived in 1946 as *New Worlds: A Fiction Magazine of the Future*, which failed in the following year. In 1948 Carnell and his group formed Nova Publications, with Wyndham as president, and *New Worlds* was relaunched in 1949, under Carnell's editorship until 1964 when he was replaced by Michael Moorcock. Its inaugural issue declared: 'From here on, the future looms ahead as a bewildering Land of If, governed by the whims and passions of individuals, by the power of Governments, by the discoveries of scientists, even by the failures and catastrophies [*sic*] which beset us'.[37] In his introduction Wyndham took the journal's commercial difficulties as evidence of the editor's commitment and declared that '*New Worlds* was founded upon the theory that science fiction is capable of dealing with matters of more general interest than cosmic cowboys and galactic gunmen'.[38] He had already demonstrated his commitment by publishing one of his stories in the second number. As we saw in the preceding chapter, 'The Living Lies' understates its setting on Venus to present an ironic parable of racism where the population is united by a common language but divided by colour indicators. This shift from interplanetary adventure to sociological analysis suggests an early sign of what became known as the New Wave in British SF.

In 1955 Wyndham published his most broad-ranging and considered article about SF called 'Science Fiction: Space-Opera' (reproduced in the Appendix) where he took bearings from

Edmund Crispin's definition that an SF story 'presupposes a technology, or an effect of technology, or a disturbance of the natural order, such as humanity, up to the time of writing, has not in actual fact experienced'.[39] Noting the inclusiveness of Crispin's definition, but not the fact that it was appearing in a mainstream publication, Wyndham went on to draw a distinction between three kinds of fiction. First, he named the 'scientific romance', though he noted that Wells had misgivings about the label even as he was establishing it. Second, he came to the 'science fiction story proper' – that is to say the type of story for which an American editor coined the term – where careful, conscientious deduction and attention to logical probability, as in the work of, say, Isaac Asimov and Arthur Clarke, are the overriding considerations. Finally, Wyndham came to the 'overwhelming mass of hackwork known as "space-opera" where any trammelling considerations of science and logic are thrown off, and anything goes so long as it is fast-moving and exciting'.[40]

Wyndham turned next to the two 'reputable ancestors' of SF – Verne and Wells. The former is summarized as a 'prophet who limited his field to technology, and disregarded the effects of its impact on society'. Wyndham fleshes out his contrast between the two writers by in effect denying Verne any status as a novelist:

> Verne, then, was a good journalist who was interested in displaying the devices that he found implicit in the new technological progress. Wells, on the other hand, wrote as a novelist interested in the effects of discoveries on people. He saw in it, moreover, opportunities for propaganda, satire, and controversy neglected by Verne. He did not break with all accepted standards to elevate novelty above the rest; rather, he took novelty and fitted it into existing patterns, and in doing this he produced a type of work which appealed, and continues to appeal, to a wider stratum of readers than the other.[41]

Verne, however, could not be discussed apart from an emerging tradition in the USA, and in a later article, Wyndham declares that Verne 'is revealed as the perfect prototype for the American science-fiction magazine story in its early stages'. He has justly become known as the 'father of science fiction' because:

> He is wonderfully inventive. He has novel ideas to convey, and to support them he uses a perfunctory framework of fiction. He

is determinedly fair with his readers, concerned to be logical (within the limits of his time's knowledge), so anxious for them to understand, that he is given to suspending the story for a time while he imparts miscellaneous items of interesting information, but more often he delivers it through the mouth of a stooge to an appreciative audience.[42]

For Wyndham, to understand the appeal of Verne's novels it is important to remember that they predated general education in a period when there were 'little means of knowing anything about science itself'.

Returning to the 1955 article, Wyndham stresses that a transatlantic line of SF derives from Verne and that 'it was then, and still is, generally true of American science fiction that the invention, the gadget, the discovery, the new twist, is its primary consideration'. The evolution of twin distinct traditions in the USA and Britain is central to Wyndham's argument and he admits that the former has become better established, for good or ill: 'It has to be remembered that science-fiction in America has now a generation of development behind it – time to build up a considerable body of conventions, taboos and jargon which become almost necessary if the same introductory ground is not to be covered again and again'.

Wyndham contrasts the cultural assumptions of the two bodies of SF readers in the following way:

> By and large, the type of story which pleases the more specialist readership (the 'fans') in America looks to English eyes ingenious, slick, mechanical, careful in argument, careless in style, and considerably weakened in holding power by lack of attention to the humanities.

Reverse the perspective and we find the following:

> By contrast, the average English story (or perhaps one should say European story) tending more towards the Wells pattern, strikes the American enthusiast as stuffy, slow, pointlessly padded out, unadventurous, and, least forgivable of all, old-fashioned in expression.[43]

Summing up his argument, Wyndham disposes of space opera and then gives his own explanation of a central characteristic of SF: 'It is space-opera that is the wild riot of pointless imaginings.

Science-fiction proper is an exercise of the imagination within known limits, and can often be a severe test of logical thought.' He even takes Wells to task for falsifying the 'consequences of his premise' in *The Food of the Gods* (1904) when describing the growth induced by this food; the full title of the novel was *The Food of the Gods and How It Came to Earth*.[44]

Having chosen a journal of education for his medium, Wyndham adopts the role of a schoolteacher in presenting his material. This article is didactic in a number of important respects, not least in addressing misconceptions of SF, for example that it is escapist or that America invented it. Wyndham includes a list of socially engaged novels ranging from Richard Jefferies's *After London* (1884), to J. D. Beresford's tale of a preternaturally gifted boy, *The Hampdenshire Wonder* (1911, US title *The Wonder*), and Edward Shanks's *The People of the Ruins* (1920), which opens with a general strike and shows its protagonist transported 150 years into the future.[45] The selection of titles is strategic. The majority are English, but some American examples are included, and Wyndham's choice suggests a broader, more nuanced version of the development of SF than his suggestion of parallel lines descending from Verne and Wells. Lastly Wyndham turns his attention to SF magazines, stressing the importance of publications like *Astounding Science Fiction* and thereby revising his rather dismissive comments elsewhere on the magazines.

During the 1950s, however, as the Cold War progressed, more and more novels were produced which engaged with the threat of nuclear war. Wyndham reviewed Nevil Shute's *On the Beach* in 1957, which famously described a community in Australia awaiting the arrival of radioactive contamination from the Northern Hemisphere after such a war. Wyndham argued that the novel succeeded partly because it hadn't been marketed under the SF label.[46] In a 1959 article for *The Listener* he further addressed nuclear war fiction, which he saw as a version of a long-established form, the 'end-of-the-world science fiction story'. He summarizes this postwar subject ironically as 'scare-'em-to-death approaches to the hypothetical World War III'. He registers a suspicion that 'the H-bomb itself may be one of those gross overstatements that alienates a reader's belief', and finds a weakness in the general direction of this fiction since, for the SF writer, 'fear he can arouse, yet it is not the fear due to conviction;

it remains uncertain, more akin to fear of the dark'. Here Wyndham rightly stresses the importance of uncertainty, but dismisses it as childish, whereas writers had been dramatizing nuclear attacks as such huge and unpredictable disasters against which there was no defence that they resembled latter-day apocalypse.

Wyndham locates a problem in the Bomb itself as subject:

> The H-bomb, in spite of its dramatic qualities and emotion-rousing factor cannot make a satisfactory protagonist. Indeed, how could it? It is a *thing*, and stories are not about things; they are about people. [Wyndham admits that authors have made efforts at representation but] the thing remains too big for them, too overwhelming, and reduces their actors to puppets. The Bomb cannot *be* the protagonist, yet it leaves no room for any other protagonist, so that it is, from a literary point of view, utterly unwieldy.

Wyndham's essay is clearly fed by memories of the Second World War, specifically of its scale in relation to bombing, and he continues that the Bomb 'is either so devastating in operation that all is destroyed, leaving nothing more to be said; or it turns out to be not quite devastating' so that the fictional warning deteriorates into a 'modified success story about how-we-beat-the-bomb'.[47]

The fictional works named by Wyndham are treated critically by him, although his evident struggles with the subject place him within the same quandary confronting the writers, namely how to conceive of the Bomb within a fictional narrative. He dismisses Mordecai Roshwald's *Level 7* (1959) as a 'paper ingenuity' and a 'bomb exercise without bombs', completely missing the point that the nuclear operative who narrates the tale – 'named' X-127 – could belong to any military bureaucracy and is distanced from the actuality of slaughter by the elaborate electronic system surrounding him. Pat Frank's *Alas, Babylon* (also 1959) comes off a little better, but again Wyndham underplays its many ironies. The action is set in the small Florida town of Fort Repose, whose inhabitants are a few of those to survive the accidental triggering of World War III. Frank dramatizes the tensions between the different survivor groups and uses his title from Revelation to draw attention to the fact that the USA has endured massive destruction at its Judgement Day. The UK author John Brunner's *The Brink* (again 1959) receives guarded praise for its depiction of a 'near-occurrence' of World War III. Here an American journalist witnesses what he assumes to be a nuclear bomb falling near him. Knocked unconscious by the detonation, when he comes to, he learns that the 'missile' was actually a space rocket which failed. Or was it? Like the other writers, Brunner draws our attention to the information gap between military and civilians. Wyndham's most positive words are reserved for Brian Aldiss's 1959 short story collection *The Canopy of Time*, which contains the nuclear subject within very few stories. It was here, however, that Wyndham found 'one of the branches which, equipped with interesting ideas, civilized habits, and a taste for words, has established itself up country, not all that far from the Ray Bradbury country'.[48] Our perspective on this review essay should be tempered when we remember that in 1955 Wyndham had made his own contribution to nuclear war fiction with *The Chrysalids*.

It was a measure of how SF was gaining status when Kingsley Amis's *New Maps of Hell* appeared in 1960, based on a series of lectures that he had given at Princeton University during 1958–1959. Much of Amis's discussion would have chimed in with Wyndham's own positions. Indeed, he is acknowledged in Amis's foreword. After admitting the sheer difficulty of defining SF, Amis does just that with the following:

> Science fiction is that class of prose narrative treating of a situation that could not arise in the world we know, but which is hypothesized on the basis of some innovation in science or technology, or pseudo-science or pseudo-technology, whether human or extra-terrestrial in origin.[49]

Like Wyndham, Amis gives special place to Verne and Wells as the 'two creators of modern science fiction', but then admits that there are other candidates and extends the pedigree of SF back to antiquity. He also stresses the need for plausibility in SF, admitting that 'whether or not an individual story does justice to the laws of nature can affect our judgement of it'. Amis also differentiates straight SF from 'space-opera', again like Wyndham, and shares the latter's perception of the American domination of the market. One of Amis's main insights is into the social function of SF when he states that 'its most important use, I submit, is a means of dramatizing social inquiry, as providing a fictional mode in which cultural tendencies can be isolated and judged'. Wyndham must have been gratified when Amis singled out his treatment of gender fantasy in 'Consider Her Ways', where a virus has killed off all men, as being 'less activist, less rambling, and far more plausible' than Charles Eric Maine's *World Without Men* (1958).[50] He would also have noticed that Amis gave extensive space to his former American agent, the writer Frederik Pohl, who with C. M. Kornbluth had written *The Space Merchants* (1952), which, Amis wrote, 'has many claims to being the best science-fiction novel so far'.[51]

For his part Wyndham returned the compliment by giving *New Maps of Hell* a very positive review in February 1961, where he praised Amis's knowledge of the field and recognized his perception that 'the development of the genre since that time [from 1926 onwards] had gone on in a kind of enclave; out of touch with general fiction' and 'unknown to the general reader'. In particular, Wyndham approved the developments described by Amis:

> the widespread replacement of the hostile and horrid invaders from space by amiable visitants anxious to assist the backward inhabitants of Earth; the trends of popular thinking as evidenced by the invention of new kinds of utopia; the fossilized attitude to sex relationships found in science fiction; the apportionment of the future between hope and fear.

And then, to clinch his approval, Wyndham quotes the same passage on the social function of SF reproduced in the preceding paragraph above. Although Amis was far less hostile to the SF label than Wyndham, he did share the other writer's perception that audiences might not appreciate contemporary fiction and film 'because they had never been told they were science fiction'.[52]

Throughout his critical writing Wyndham showed a sharp awareness of the state of the market for SF, and between 1959 and 1968 he produced some 21 book reports for his UK publisher Michael Joseph. These reports covered works like Poul Anderson's *Twilight World* (1961), Robert Sheckley's *Journey*

Beyond Tomorrow (1962) and Walter Tevis's *The Man Who Fell to Earth* (1963).

In his last published essay, 'Has Science Fiction a Future?' (1969), Wyndham returns yet again to the issue of the SF label dating from the 1920s. He explains it as a 'trade-name coined by publishers' distributors to classify a then new type of magazine', which has persisted despite being such an incompetent classifier. It's unclear whether this was editorial planning or Wyndham's initiative, but the article appeared under a collage of the leading SF magazines, chronologically from left to right, ending with the Penguin edition of *The Day of the Triffids*.[53] Wyndham burlesques 'science fiction' as a catch-all including anything from the 'first chapter of Genesis to the works of Edgar Rice Burroughs, the book of Revelation, the fantasies of J.R.R. Tolkien, *1984*, and the adventures of Superman'.[54] He includes a rare reference to Nigel Kneale's scientist Quatermass from his 1950s films.[55]

As usual, Wyndham breaks SF down into a hierarchy of sub-genres, starting with the 'cartoon strip and the horror film', where he ironically lists their features as a stock list of features:

> They are in the main concerned with maidens, sexy, heroes to the rescue of; super-brains, unlimited power of; monsters, vast, destruction of; women, hell-cat type, sadistic bents of; males, tom-cat type, conquering powers of;

And he concludes by remarking that these 'hardy constants' will probably persist in the foreseeable future with minor variations for fashion. After an ironic glance at how in space-opera the 'Americans have been dispersing cowboys and Indians throughout the galaxy', Wyndham turns to one of his central purposes, to explain the 'science science-fiction story' as a 'combination of playground and think-box for scientists themselves. It can be highly intelligent, often beyond the grasp of non-scientists, and fascinating in its assumptions. It is usually populated by lay-figures, for the idea is the thing that matters, and it is little interested in literary standards'. When he turns to the 'story proper', i.e. the SF story with literary pretentions, instead of giving a definition, Wyndham challenges the reader: 'would you call Aldous Huxley a "science fiction writer" on the strength of *Brave New World*?' His point is partly historical because he flags up writers like Bernard Shaw, William Morris and Samuel Butler, whose works predate the currency of the SF label, and partly an invitation to us readers to examine what we understand by 'science fiction'. Are we, for instance, such purists that we would exclude from consideration Wells's *The First Men in the Moon* or *The Food of the Gods* on 'on the ground that they are not scientifically viable'?

In case we are reading this as a conservative message, Wyndham cites contemporary narratives by writers like Arthur C. Clarke, John Christopher, Brian Aldiss, John Brunner and J. G. Ballard, whose works would fit the SF label were it not for the associations that would carry with 'space-opera' and 'space-horror'. A major recent development he notes is the impetus to 'promote "s-f" to an art-form'. As part of the latter he rather gingerly mentions 'something called "inner-space"'.[56] The allusion here is to Ballard's famous 1962 essay 'Which Way to Inner Space?' where he insists: 'it is inner space, not outer, that needs to be explored.' Turning away from the then current Space Race, he recommended a rejection of 'rocket ships and ray guns' in favour of 'more psycho-literary ideas'.[57] The following year he presented 'inner space' as 'the internal landscape of tomorrow that is a transmuted image of the past'. Wyndham would no doubt have applauded Ballard's replacement of the SF label with that of 'speculative fantasy' which shares characteristics with surrealist art, a genre gathering importance 'in the century of Hiroshima and Cape Canaveral'.[58]

By the time Wyndham published his essay, debate was already widespread over what constituted the New Wave in British SF. The label was first applied to SF by the American writer and critic P. Schuyler Miller, who in a review column of 1961 when discussing John Carnell and *New Worlds* wrote: 'It's a moot question whether Carnell discovered the "big names" of British science fiction – Wyndham, Clarke, Russell, Christopher – or whether they discovered him. Whatever the answer, there is no question at all about the "new wave"'.[59] Miller stressed that he thought Carnell hadn't received the credit due him in the USA. Subsequent criticism has agreed that *New Worlds* played a crucial role for New Wave SF, particularly once Michael Moorcock took over the editorship in 1964, but it is important to see that Wyndham was already being recognized as soon as the new term was being introduced.

Although the discussion of the New Wave has tended to concentrate on the 1960s, Carnell had laid important groundwork throughout the previous decade in moving away from conventional SF methods and subjects, as J. G, Ballard later recognized when he declared: 'Carnell's role is central to the transformation of modern science fiction' and noted that 'among those who were sympathetic in those very early days were John Brunner and John Wyndham'.[60] When Carnell handed over the editorship of *New Worlds* to Michael Moorcock in 1964, the latter signalled the change in an editorial which called for 'A New Literature for the Space Age', proposing William Burroughs as an instructive figure of change.[61] For its stylistic inventiveness and anti-establishment subjects, the SF of the sixties has tended to be identified with the New Wave at the expense of the preceding decade, and of course the very title of *New Worlds* carried a call for novelty as soon as it was launched. The changes in sixties SF were fed partly by generational distrust and partly by changes in publishing,[62] and critical commentary on Wyndham's fiction of the 1950s has increasingly come to recognize its complex interrogation of British culture.[63] Right from the 1930s and throughout his career, he had attempted to situate his practice and perceptions of SF in contrast with those operating in the USA.

Notes

INTRODUCTION

1 David Ketterer, 'Introduction', *Plan for Chaos*, p. 9. The novels were *Trouble at Hanard* (1948), *Confusion at Campden Trig* (also 1948), *One Thing Constant* (1949) and *Song for a Siren* (1951). He also wrote one SF novel, unpublished, called *Son of the Morning*.

2 Harris, 1999, p. 21.

3 Harris, 1999, pp. 25, 36.

4 Letter to Pohl of 3 April 1950, quoted in Binns, 2019, p. 198.

5 Letter of 6 December 1952, Binns, 2019, p. 218. The 2005 film was directed by Mick Conefrey.

6 'Introduction', Edmund Crispin, ed. *Best SF. Science Fiction Stories* (London: Faber & Faber, 1955). In addition to Wyndham, the first collections included stories by Isaac Asimov, Ray Bradbury, Brian Aldiss and Arthur C. Clarke.

7 A detailed report of the convention (with photographs of Wyndham) can be found at *THEN* Archive – 1957. Carnell went on to edit a series of anthologies with the title *New Writings in SF* from 1964 to 1977.

8 'Sir. Arthur Charles Clarke' (2008), at http://www.neo-forum.com/sir-arthur-charles-clarke_topic12280.html/. From 1946, Clarke, Wyndham, John Christopher and other SF enthusiasts met regularly in the White Horse pub in London, commemorated in Clarke's *Tales from the White Hart* (New York: Ballantine Books, 1957).

9 '1960: Tonight – John Wyndham', *BBC*, https://www.bbc.co.uk/archive/tonight--john-wyndham/z7368xs/. The programme was broadcast on 6 September 1960, shortly after the publication of *Trouble with Lichen*.

10 The participants were Brian Aldiss, Kingsley Amis, J. G. Ballard, John Brunner, Kenneth Bulmer, John Carnell, and Wyndham. The programme was broadcast on 18 March 1962.

NOTES

11 For a survey of movie adaptations, see Sawyer, 1999.
12 The passage appeared on the back cover of the 1963 Penguin edition of *Trouble with Lichen*. The review appeared in the *Observer*.
13 Amis, 1961, p. 63; 'John Wyndham on Science Fiction: Props for Comment', 1961, p. 173.
14 Aldiss, 1986, p. 253. The Wyndham scholar David Ketterer has explained the major fiction from 1951 to 1960 as a sequence articulating Wyndham's fear of women and sexuality: 'John Wyndham: The Facts of Life Sextet' (2005). On the general interrelation between knowledge, expertise and society, see Rees, 2019.
15 Stephen King, *Danse Macabre* (London: Macdonald, 1981), chapter 2: Margaret Atwood, afterword to 2015 edition of *Chocky*; Jeff VanderMeer, introduction to 2022 Modern Library edition of *The Day of the Triffids*.
16 For information, see Sawyer, 'The Wyndham Archives', 1998; and 'Special Collections & Archives: The Return of the Triffids', https://libguides.liverpool.ac.uk/library/sca/wyndhamexhib/.

CHAPTER 1: PREWAR

1 Ketterer, 'Vivisection', 1999, p. 76.
2 Gernsback's editorials have been collected in *The Perversity of Things: Hugo Gernsback on Media, Tinkering and Scientifiction*, ed. Grant Wythoff (Minneapolis: University of Minnesota Press, 2016).
3 Hugo Gernsback, 'Wonders of Technology', *Wonder Stories* 4.x (March 1933), p. 741. Valuable commentary on the SF magazines of this period can be found in Mike Ashley's *The Time Machines* (2000).
4 Cheng, 2012, p. 46.
5 Quoted in Ashley, 2000, p. 73.
6 *Scientifiction* 1.ii (April 1937), pp. 3–4.
7 Ibid., p. 12.
8 A name possibly borrowed from Gladys Mitchell's mystery novels which feature the polymath detective Lestrange Bradley.
9 *Sleepers of Mars*, p. 65.
10 Ibid., p. 68.
11 Ibid., p. 65.
12 H. G. Wells, 'The Man of the Year Million: A Scientific Forecast', in Stephen Arata, ed. *The Time Machine* (New York: Norton, 2009), p. 140.
13 *Wonder Stories* 5.v (December 1933), 1353.
14 *Exiles on Asperus*, p. 96.
15 *Wanderers of Time*, p. 9.
16 Ibid., p. 17.

NOTES

17 *Sleepers of Mars*, p. 118.

18 Wyndham may have had in mind the 1896 volume *Might is Right or, The Survival of the Fittest*, by Ragnar Redbeard (probably Arthur Desmond), which argued that sheer strength carried its own moral sanction as a 'natural law'.

19 *Wanderers of Time*, p. 138.

20 Ibid., p. 158.

21 In his introduction to the revised 1964 Lancer Books edition of the novel, Wyndham notes the withdrawal of France and Italy from north Africa and early signs of his characters' 'propensity towards continued chatter' (p. 6).

22 *The Best of John Wyndham: 1932–1949*, p. 20.

23 Ibid., p. 36.

24 About 'The Lost Machine' and other stories, Mike Ashley has written that Wyndham was 'much more sympathetic to his characters, especially aliens, and I think this portrayed a more British attitude unlike most American writers who wrote with a more active frontier spirit', quoted in Binns, 2019, p. 86.

25 Serialized in *The Passing Show*, 2 May–20 June 1936. Also serialized as *The Space Machine* in *Modern Wonder*, 22 May–24 July 1937.

26 *The Passing Show* (2 May, 1936), p. 40.

27 The inclusion of an active intelligent female character in this fiction was so unusual for its period that in 'The Lost Machine', the editor of *Amazing Stories* changed Joan's name to John.

28 'Sleepers of Mars' first appeared in *Tales of Wonder* for Spring 1938, then as the title novella in the 1973 Coronet collection.

29 *Sleepers of Mars*, p. 9.

30 *Sleepers of Mars*, p. 34.

31 *Exiles on Asperus*, p. 23.

32 Ibid., p. 60.

33 *The Best of John Wyndham: 1932–1949*, p. 30.

34 'Introduction', ibid., p. 9.

35 Ibid., p. 20.

36 Ibid., p. 17.

37 *Sleepers of Mars*, p. 139 (as 'The Man from Earth').

38 'Why Blame Wells?', *Fantasy Review* 2 (December 1948–January 1949), p. 15.

39 *Fantasy* was edited by T. Stanhope Sprigg. In addition to Wyndham, it carried stories by Eric Frank Russell, John Russell Fearn and S. Fowler Wright. For commentary, see Ashley, 2000, pp. 131–132.

40 'Judson's Annihilator', *Amazing Stories* 13.x (October 1939), p. 104.

41 'Judson's Annihilator', p. 134.

42 *Wanderers of Time*, p. 85.

NOTES

43 'Meet the Authors', *Amazing Stories*, 13.x (October 1939), p. 146; discussed in Binns, 2019, pp. 95–96.

44 For details on Wyndham's wartime experiences, see Binns, 2019, chapters 5–8.

CHAPTER 2: TRIFFIDS AND OTHER INVASIONS

1 V. Ketterer, 'John Wyndham's World War III' (2012).

2 A comet features as a means of social control in John Christopher's *The Year of the Comet* (1955).

3 Critical reactions to the impact of the triffids have varied. Manlove (1991) notes the hollowing out of values, while Gochenour (2011) sees Wyndham as stressing the material conditions of ecological balance.

4 *Weird Tales*, April 1930. The serialization of *Triffids* in *Collier's* carried the title 'The Revolt of the Triffids'.

5 *Wonder Stories*, June 1935.

6 *Wanderers of Time*, p. 138.

7 On possible sources, see Ketterer, 'The Genesis of the Triffids', 2004.

8 'And the Green Grass Grew ...' *Fantasy Review* 3 (Summer 1949), pp. 21–22.

9 Hart, 1960.

10 Harris, 1999, p. 42.

11 Luckhurst, 2005, p. 132.

12 The 'three-legged principle' of locomotion echoes that applied in Wyndham's 1937 story 'The Perfect Creature' ('Una') as being more efficient than human motion. Here an experimental biologist redesigns the human form, correcting its weaknesses.

13 On these colonial analogies, see Maatta, 2020.

14 For a full account of the different versions of *Triffids*, see Stock, 2015.

15 For valuable commentary on their complex ecosystem as human-created organisms, see Gochenour, 2011.

16 For comparisons between the two novels, see Hurst, 1986a and 1986b.

17 Cf. Maatta, 2017.

18 Ruddick, 1993, p. 141.

19 Simon Clark's *The Night of the Triffids* (London: Hodder & Stoughton, 2001) is a sequel narrated by Masen's son David, set partly on the Isle of Wight and partly in Manhattan. Other sequels are Simon Gould's *The Land of the Triffids* (2016) and John Whitbourn's *The Age of the Triffids* (2020).

20 John Christopher, *The Death of Grass* (London: Michael Joseph, 1956), p. 135.

NOTES

21 Cf. Matthews, 2016.

22 Ketterer, 2009, p. 2.

23 Wyndham's original title comes from Act 1 of Bernard Shaw's *Man and Superman* (1903), where a character (male) declares: 'vitality in a woman is a blind fury of creation'.

24 *Plan for Chaos*, 2009, p. 148.

25 Binns, 2019, pp. 189–190.

26 On the gendering of Phyllis' role, see Walton, 2009.

27 Letter of 21 May 1951, Binns, 2019, pp. 217–218.

28 *Kraken* was apparently considered by Nigel Kneale for TV adaptation; Andy Murray, *Into the Unknown: The Fantastic Life of Nigel Kneale* (London: Headpress, 2017), p. 112.

29 For a reading of the novel in relation to hazardous waste disposal, see Smith, 1991.

30 Seidel, 2022.

31 Wyndham could also have known of F. H. Mackintosh's account of geological subsidence in 'England is Sinking!' (*Discovery: A Monthly Popular Journal of Knowledge* (April 1938), 13–16), where the Thames Embankment functions as a measure of water levels.

32 In the Michael Joseph proofs; Pollard, 2018.

33 'Monsters May Be Real!' *Sunday Pictorial* (14 January 1962).

34 Place names are very rare in the novel, Rigo (for Rigolet), Waknuk (for Wabush) occur, but naming would contextualize the opening settlement within the world, which the regime resists.

35 Wyndham may have taken a cue for his title from Raymond Z. Gallun's story 'The Lunar Chrysalis', describing interaction between the Earth and Moon, which appeared in *Amazing Stories* for September 1931. One manuscript version of the novel carries the title *Time for a Change*.

36 *Argosy* 16.ix (September 1955), pp. 111–112.

37 These critics include Krome (2015), Priyadarsini (2022) and Downey (2023).

38 Wymer, 1992.

39 Hart, 1960.

40 Henry Kuttner, *Mutant* (London: Weidenfeld & Nicolson, 1962), p. 224. Italics in original.

41 See for example Wagner, 2004 and Stock, 2016.

42 Cf. Wagner, 2004.

43 Atwood, 2015.

44 Atwood, 2015. For details of the textual differences between UK and US editions, see Ketterer, 2017.

45 The actors are also multi-ethnic, reflecting the transformation of English society since the 1950s.

46 Tisdall, 2021; 2022.

NOTES

47 Thomas Henry Huxley, *Discourses Biological and Geological* (1894), Chpater 8: 'Biogenesis and Abiogenesis'.

48 The novels were *Dawn* (1987), *Adulthood Rites* (1988) and *Imago* (1989). They were later known as the Lilith's Brood trilogy.

49 'Roar of Rockets!', Sawyer, 2021, p. 192.

50 For discussion of the othering of the children, see Bruhm, 2016 and Hansen, 2022.

51 The film, directed by Wolf Rilla, was originally planned to be set in the USA but, partly after it ran into difficulties with the Catholic League of Decency, production moved to Britain and most of the film was shot in a village near Watford. A further adaptation called *Children of the Damned* followed in 1964 and *Village of the Damned* (set in California) in 1995. For commentary on these film adaptations, see Sawyer, 1999.

52 Sawyer, 2005.

CHAPTER 3: PERMUTATIONS OF SCIENCE FICTION

1 'New Worlds Profile: John Wyndham', *New Worlds* Vol. 24 no. 70 (April 1958), inside front cover. The profile announced 'four new novelettes by John Wyndham, written with a rather different approach to his usual style. They are so close to reality they could almost be true'.

2 For a discussion of its impact see Paul Dickson, *Sputnik: The Shock of the Century* (New York: Walker, 2001).

3 Carnell 1958, p. 3. Carnell was partly endorsing and publicizing Arthur Hale's article 'Science Fiction and the Space Age' in the US journal *Publishers Weekly*.

4 Arthur C. Clarke, *How the World Was One: The Turbulent History of Global Communications* (London: Victor Gollancz, 1993), pp. 168–174. The stories were collected in *The Other Side of the Sky* (1958).

5 'Personally Speaking', *News of the World* (16 September 1966), p. 11.

6 Oppenheimer applied his description to the Trinity Test of the atomic bomb in New Mexico during July 1945. His description was subsequently adopted by Rober Jungk for his 1956 history of the atomic project.

7 Binns, 2019, chapter 12.

8 In 2015 the biochemist Alistair Miller read *Trouble with Lichen* and was so impressed that he named his own molecular innovation company Darr House after Saxover's centre.

9 Raisborough and Watkins, 2021.

10 Atwood, 2015, 'Introduction'.

11 The March 1963 number of *Amazing Stories* where *Chocky* first

NOTES

appeared included an article by the US novelist Ben Bova on 'Intelligent Life in Space'.

12 *Web* (London: Penguin, 1980), p. 9.

13 Grover Smith, ed. *The Letters of Aldous Huxley* (London: Chatto & Windus, 1969), p. 348; George Wickes and Raymond Fraser, 'Aldous Huxley, The Art of Fiction No. 24', *Paris Review* 23 (Spring 1960) online.

14 For an interpretation of the novel as a complex investigation of decolonization, see Oliver-Hobley, 2022.

15 She also alludes to the 'life-force' from Shaw's *Back to Methuselah*, one of Wyndham's recurring reference points in evolutionary theory.

16 John Hammond, ed., *The Complete Short Stories of H. G. Wells* (London: Phoenix Press, 2000), pp. 441, 442.

17 Wyndham's most likely source on the island would have been Arthur Grimble, colonial administrator of the Gilbert and Ellice Islands, and author of the bestsellers *A Pattern of Islands* (1952) and *Return to the Islands* (1957); (Oliver-Hobley, 2022).

CHAPTER 4: *CONSIDER HER WAYS* AND OTHER STORIES

1 'Editorial', *New Worlds* 1.i (July 1946), p. 23.

2 Aldiss, 1986, p. 298.

3 In the December 1956 issue of *New Worlds*.

4 Carnell, 1950, p. 37.

5 'The Living Lies', p. 10.

6 'The Living Lies', p. 17.

7 'Introduction', *The Best from 'New Worlds' Science Fiction* (London: T.V. Boardman, 1955), pp. 8, 7.

8 'Fantasies and Facts', *Science-Fantasy* 1.i (Summer 1950), p. 3.

9 Possibly suggested by the character of Octavia in Robert Graves's 1934 historical novel *I, Claudius*.

10 Wyndham's history machine was partly realized when Internet Archive launched their 'Wayback Machine' in 2001.

11 *Amazing Stories* 15.iii (March 1941), p. 113.

12 'Operation Peep', *Science-Fantasy* 1.iii (Winter 1951–2), p. 4. Charles Fort (1874–1932) published four books of anomalous ('Fortean') phenomena: *The Book of the Damned* (1919), *New Lands* (1923), *Lo!* (1931) and *Wild Talents* (1932). A Fortean Society was founded in 1931, which included among its members Eric Frank Russell. When Wyndham's story was collected in *The Seeds of Time* the reference to Fort was dropped and cultural identifiers changed from American to British.

NOTES

13 In *The Seeds of Time* the capitals are replaced with italics, losing the effect of boosterism.

14 'The Pattern of Science Fiction', p. 3.

15 'Foreword', p. 1.

16 For a listing of the *Best SF* contents, see isfdb.org/cgi-bin/pe.cgi?24864.

17 Edmund Crispin, 'Introduction', *Best SF: Science Fiction Stories* (London: Faber, 1955).

18 'Una' in *Best SF2* (described as 'delightful nonsense' in the introduction) and 'Consider Her Ways' (as 'Sometime, Never') in *Best SF5*. Apart from Wyndham, the most frequent authors anthologized were Brian Aldiss, Eric Frank Russell, Ray Bradbury and Fredric Brown.

19 *The Best of John Wyndham 1951–1960*, p. 38.

20 Arthur C. Clarke, *The Sands of Mars* (London: Sphere, 1969), p. 9.

21 *The Best of John Wyndham 1951–1960*, p. 67.

22 'Jizzle' was adapted for the series *Alfred Hitchcock Presents* and broadcast in 1961, having been co-written with John Collier, whose fiction Wyndham greatly admired. Indeed *Collier's* 1951 collection *Fancies and Goodnights* may well have suggested a model for *Jizzle*.

23 *Jizzle* (London: New English Library, 1973), p. 62.

24 Wyndham's title draws on the line from Act 3 of *King Lear*, 'More Sinned Against Than Sinning'.

25 'Consider Her Ways' was first published in *Sometime Never: Three Tales of Imagination* (1956), which also included William Golding's 'Envoy Extraordinary' and Mervyn Peake's 'Boy in Darkness'.

26 Binns, 2019, p. 247.

27 *Galaxy Science Fiction* 27 (December 1968), p. 114. The story carried a header opening 'Where there's a will, there's a female way'.

28 The Life Force is taken from Bernard Shaw's 1903 play *Man and Superman*, where it figures as an evolutionary impulse.

CHAPTER 5. WYNDHAM ON SF

1 'Fantasia', 'What "S.F." Means in U.S.', *Scientifiction* 1.ii (April 1937), p. 4.

2 'Sock Him Fans – He Can Take It!', *Scientifiction* 1.iv (August 1937), pp. 6–7, 10.

3 'He's Converting the Masses!', *Scientifiction* 1.i (January 1937), p. 6.

4 Ibid., p. 8. Capek's novel was reviewed with J. S. Bradford's *Even a Worm*, which narrates a general revolt by animals against their human masters.

5 *Scientifiction* 1.iii, p. 12.

NOTES

6 'Why This Cosmic Wild West Stuff?' *Scientifiction* 1.ii (April 1937), p. 12.

7 *Scientifiction* 1.iv, p. 11.

8 'The Flame That Went Out', *Fantasy Review* 2.vii (June–July 1948), p. 9.

9 'Publishers' Plans for Science Fiction', *Fantasy Review* 1.i (Feb.–Mar. 1947), p. 2.

10 'Slave to the Fantastic', *Fantasy Review* 1.i (Feb.–Mar. 1947), p. 10.

11 'The Incomplete Machen', *Fantasy Review* 2.xii (December 1948–January 1949), p. 23.

12 '...And Other Expositions', *Fantasy Review* 2.vii (Feb.-Mar. 1948), p. 13.

13 Gerald Heard, *The Great Fog and Other Weird Tales* (London: Cassell, 1947), p. 27.

14 Ibid., p. 33.

15 'The Fate of the First Men', *Fantasy Review* 1.v (October-November 1947), p. 12.

16 'Satirical Salad', *Fantasy Review* 1.v (October–November 1947), p. 14.

17 'And the Green Grass Grew...', *Fantasy Review* 3.xv (Summer 1949), pp. 30–31.

18 'Doomsday in Moronia', *Science-Fantasy Review* 4.xviii (Spring 1950), pp. 30–31.

19 Ibid. In Autumn 1949 the journal was re-titled. Wyndham may be alluding in his title to Eleanor Rowland Wembridge's 'The People of Moronia', which appeared in *The American Mercury* for January 1926.

20 'Sowing New Thoughts', *Tales of Wonder* 7 (Summer 1939), pp. 124–125. The journal was edited by Walter Gillings, who in his editorial for the third number on 'The Evolution of Science Fiction' recognized that the USA had developed and popularized the scientific romance started by Wells.

21 'The Flame That Went Out', *Fantasy Review* vol. 2 no. 9 (June–July 1948), pp. 8–9.

22 'Why Blame Wells?' *Fantasy Review* 2.xii (December 1948–January 1949), p. 14. It was a measure of the politicization of SF that this issue reprinted a Soviet article attacking Raymond F. Jones and Western writers generally for being the 'fascistic' lackeys of Wall Street.

23 Ibid., p. 15.

24 Ibid., p. 15. Comstockery was a form of censorship based on perceived immorality, named after the secretary of the New York Society for the Suppression of Vice, Anthony Comstock.

25 'Not So Simple', *Authentic Science Fantasy Monthly* vol. 1, no. 30 (February 1953), pp. 30–31.

NOTES

26 'The Pattern of Science Fiction', *Science-Fantasy* 3.vii (March 1954), pp. 2–4.

27 'Roar of the Rockets!', Sawyer, 2021, p. 190.

28 'Will This Hasten the Death of the Detective Thriller?' *W. H. Smith & Sons Trade Circular* (1951).

29 Ibid., p. 181.

30 Ibid., pp. 192, 193.

31 'No Science Fiction This', *Smith's Trade News* 1765 (21 September 1957), p. 37.

32 'The Scientific Novel', *The Author* 68 (Summer 1958), p. 90.

33 'Science Fiction: The Facts', *TV Times* 347 (22 July 962), p. 11.

34 'Introduction', *The Best from 'New Worlds' Science Fiction*, pp. 7, 10–11.

35 'New Worlds Profiles: John Carnell', *New Worlds* vol. 12, no. 35 (May 1955). The issue also carried Wyndham's story 'Compassion Circuit'.

36 'Ted' Carnell, 'The Magazine That Nearly Was', *Before Nova Publications*, 1940 mimeograph, https://fiawol.org.uk//FanStuff/THEN%20Archive/NewWorlds/1940NW01.htm.

37 'Editorial', *New Worlds* 1.i (July 1946), p. 22.

38 'Introduction', p. 12.

39 Edmund Crispin, ed. *Best SF: Science Fiction Stories* (London: Faber, 1955). Edmund Crispin was the pen name of the English crime novelist Robert Bruce Montgomery. The anthology included stories by Ray Bradbury, John Christopher, Eric Frank Russell and Wyndham himself. The Montgomery papers in the Bodleian Library include correspondence with Wyndham. See Appendix.

40 'Science Fiction: Space-Opera', *The Preparatory School Review* (October 1955), p. 6.

41 Ibid., pp. 7, 8.

42 'John Wyndham on Science Fiction: Verne Revisited', *John O'London's Weekly* 5 (6 July 1961), p. 13.

43 'Science Fiction: Space-Opera', pp. 7, 8. The penultimate paragraph may include a glance at the American magazines like *Harper's* and *Vanity Fair* which became known as the 'slicks' in the 1930s.

44 In his 1934 preface to *Seven Famous Novels*, Wells himself described the book as a 'fantasia on the change of scale in human affairs'.

45 Beresford's novel may have served as part-inspiration for *The Midwich Cuckoos* and Shanks's description of a deserted London resembles the opening scenes of *The Day of the Triffids*.

46 'No Science Fiction This', p. 36.

47 'Science Fiction', *The Listener*, vol. 62, no. 1601 (3 December 1959), p. 999.

48 Ibid., p. 1001.

49 Kingsley Amis, *New Maps of Hell: A Survey of Science Fiction* (London:

NOTES

Faber, 1961), p. 18. Amis dedicated his study to Robert Montgomery, aka Edmund Crispin, whose 1950 anthology Wyndham had cited in his 1955 article.

50 Ibid., pp. 21, 63, 91.

51 Ibid., p. 124. Amis reviewed Wyndham's *The Trouble with Lichen* in *The Observer* on 16 October 1960.

52 'John Wyndham on Science Fiction: Props for Comment', *John O'London's Weekly* 5 (16 February 1961), p. 173.

53 The magazines are in order *Amazing Stories, Astounding Science Fiction, Nebula, New Worlds, Fantasy and Science Fiction, Galaxy,* and *Analog.*

54 'Has Science Fiction a Future?' *Radio Times* 182 (30 January 1969), pp. 27–28.

55 He appeared in *The Quatermass Experiment* (1953) and in the subsequent serials *Quatermass II* (1955) and *Quatermass and the Pit* (1958–1959).

56 'Has Science Fiction a Future?', pp. 27–28.

57 Ibid.

58 J. G. Ballard, *Selected Nonfiction 1962–2007,* ed. Mark Blacklock (Cambridge MA: MIT Press, 2023), pp. 3–7. J. G. Ballard, 'Time, Memory and Inner Space', *A User's Guide to the Millennium: Essays and Reviews* (London: Harper Collins, 1996), pp. 199–201.

59 P. Schuyler Miller, 'The Reference Library', *Analog Science Fact & Science Fiction* 68.iii (November 1961), p. 167.

60 J. G. Ballard in his 1974 review of Brian Aldiss's *Billion Year Spree, Selected Nonfiction*), p. 189.

61 Michael Moorcock, 'A New Literature for the Space Age', *New Worlds* 142 (May–June 1964), pp. 2–3.

62 For generational distrust see Luckhurst, 2005. For changes in publishing see Latham, 2017.

63 See Hubble, 2005; Falkner, 2017.

Bibliography

WORKS BY JOHN WYNDHAM

[John Wyndham Parkes Lucas Beynon Harris published under the following pen names: John Beynon Harris (JBH), John Beynon (JB), Lucas Parkes and Wyndham Parkes (WP). Unless otherwise indicated works appeared as by John Wyndham. Note: This bibliography draws throughout on the work of the Wyndham scholar David Ketterer and the bibliography of Phil Stephenson-Payne]

A1. *The Curse of the Burdens*, JBH (London: Aldine Press, 1927).
A2. *The Secret People*, JB (London: George Newnes, 1935; London: Penguin, 2016). Serialized in *The Toronto Star Weekly* (23 May–25 July 1936 with introduction by JW.
A3. *Foul Play Suspected*, JB (London: George Newnes, 1935; New York: Modern Library, 2023).
A4. *Stowaway to Mars*. As *Planet Plane*, by JB (London: George Newnes, 1936), Serialized under the title 'Stowaway to Mars' in *The Passing Show* and thereafter known as *Stowaway to Mars*. (London: Penguin, 2016). Also published as *The Space Machine*.
A5. *The Day of the Triffids* (London: Michael Joseph, 1951; London: Penguin, 1954). Abridgement serialized as 'Revolt of the Triffids' in *Collier's* (6 January –3 February 1951).
A6. *The Kraken Wakes* (London: Michael Joseph, 1953; London: Penguin, 1955). Abridged and with different ending as *Out of the Deeps* (New York: Ballantine, 1953).
A7. *Jizzle* (stories) (London: Denis Dobson, 1954).
A8. *The Chrysalids*. As *Re-Birth* (New York: Ballantine, 1955). (London: Michael Joseph, 1955; London: Penguin, 1958). Abridgement in *Argosy* 16 (September–October 1955).

BIBLIOGRAPHY

A9. *The Seeds of Time* (stories) (London: Michael Joseph, 1956; London: Penguin, 1961).

A10. *Tales of Gooseflesh and Laughter* (stories) (New York: Ballantine, 1956).

A11. *The Midwich Cuckoos* (London: Michael Joseph, 1957; London: Penguin, 1960).

A12. *The Infinite Moment* (stories) (New York: Ballantine, 1961).

A13. *The Outward Urge* (story sequence) as by JW and Lucas Parkes (London: Michael Joseph, 1959; London: Penguin, 1962).

A14. *Trouble with Lichen* (London: Michael Joseph, 1960; London: Penguin, 1963).

A15. *Consider Her Ways and Others* (stories) (London: Michael Joseph, 1961; London: Penguin, 1963). 'Odd' collected in A30.

A16. *John Wyndham Omnibus* [*The Day of the Triffids, The Kraken Wakes, The Chrysalids*] (London: Michael Joseph, 1964).

A17. *Chocky* (London: Michael Joseph, 1968; London: Penguin, 1970).

A18. *Sleepers of Mars* (stories), as by John Beynon (London: Coronet Books, 1973).

A19. *Wanderers of Time* (stories), as by John Beynon (London: Coronet Books, 1973).

A20. *The Best of John Wyndham*, ed. Angus Wells (London: Sphere Books, 1973).

A21. *The Best of John Wyndham 1932–1949* (London: Sphere Books, 1974).

A22. *The Best of John Wyndham 1951–1960* (London: Sphere Books, 1977).

A23. *Exiles on Asperus* (stories) (London: Coronet Books, 1979).

A24. *Web* (London: Michael Joseph, 1979; London: Penguin, 1980).

A25. *John Wyndham Omnibus* (London: Book Club Associates, 1981); A5, A6, A8, A9, A14, A11.

A26. *Meteor and Other Stories* (simplified) (Oxford: Oxford University Press, 1991).

A27. *No Place Like Earth* (stories), introduction by John Pelan (Seattle: Darkside Press, 2003). First publication of 'Blackmail'.

A28. *Plan for Chaos*, ed. David Ketterer and Andy Sawyer (Liverpool: Liverpool University Press, 2009; London: Penguin, 2010).

A29. *Logical Fantasy: The Many Worlds of John Wyndham*, ed. David Dyte (Clawson MI: Subterranean Press, 2024).

A30. *Technical Slip: Collected Stories* (A7 and A1) (New York: Random House, 2024).

BIBLIOGRAPHY

STORIES

'Vivisection', by JBH. *The Bee: An Independent Journal of Art, Literature, Political Science and Music* 1 (November 1919), 29–30. See below under Ketterer 1999.

'Worlds to Barter', by JBH, *Wonder Stories* 2.xii (May 1931), 1422–1439. Collected in A18.

'The Lost Machine', by JBH, *Amazing Stories* 7.i (April 1932), 40–47. Collected in A21, A30.

'The Venus Adventure', by JBH, *Wonder Stories* 3.xii (May 1932), 1352–1373, 1379; by JB in *Tales of Wonder* 7 (Summer 1939), 4–41, 53. Collected in A23.

'The Stare', by JBH, *Daily Express* (15 November 1932), 12.

'Wanderers of Time', by JBH, *Wonder Stories* 4.x (March 1933), 779–796. By JB in *Tales of Wonder* 13 (Winter 1941), 6–35, 53. Collected in A19.

'The Third Vibrator', by JBH, *Wonder Stories* 4.xii (May 1933), 938–945; *Tales of Wonder* 4 (Autumn 1938), 94–104. Collected in A18.

'The Puff-Ball Menace', by JBH originally as 'Spheres of Hell', *Wonder Stories* 5.iii (October 1933), 231–239; retitled by JB in *Tales of Wonder* 3 (Summer 1938), 51–67. Collected in A19, A30.

'Invisible Monster', by JBH, *Wonder Stories* 5.v (December 1933), 448–465; by JB in *Tales of Wonder* 11 (Summer 1940), 6–23. Collected in A18.

'Exiles on Asperus', by JBH, *Wonder Stories Quarterly* 4.ii.iv (Winter 1933), 166–187. Collected in A23.

'The Moon Devils', by JBH, *Wonder Stories* 5.ix (April 1934), 968–979; *Tales of Wonder* 3 (June 1938), 95–107. Collected as 'The Last Lunarians' in A19.

'The Man from Beyond', by JBH, *Wonder Stories* 6.iv (September 1934), 420–435, 492; *Tales of Wonder* 10 (March 1940), 3–59. Collected in A21, A30 and as 'The Man from Earth' in A18.

'The Cathedral Crypt', by JBH, *Marvel Tales* 1 (March/April 1935), 164–170.

'The Perfect Creature', by JB, *Tales of Wonder* 1 (June 1937), 116–127. Also reprinted under the title 'Female of the Species' in *Argosy* (October 1953). Collected in A7 and A10 as 'Una' and A21 as 'Perfect Creature'.

'Sleepers of Mars', by JB, *Tales of Wonder* 2 (Spring 1938), 4–39. Collected in A18.

'Beyond the Screen', by JB, *Fantasy: A Magazine of Thrilling Science Fiction* 1 (August 1938), 92–128, and A30. As 'Judson's Annihilator', *Amazing Stories* 13. x (October 1939), 104–135.

'The Trojan Beam', by JB, *Fantasy: A Magazine of Thrilling Science Fiction* 2 (March 1939), 60–77. Collected in A21.

129

BIBLIOGRAPHY

'Derelict of Space', by JB, *Fantasy: A Magazine of Thrilling Science Fiction* 3 (June 1939), 2–20. Collected in A19, A27.

'Child of Power', by WP, *Fantasy: A Magazine of Thrilling Science Fiction* 3 (June 1939), 89, 90–105. Collected in A19, A30.

'Praise Famous Men', by JB, *Lilliput* 5. iii (September 1939), 288–289.

'Vengeance by Proxy', by JB, *Strange Stories* 3 (February 1940), 48–54. Collected in A21.

'Phoney Meteor', by JB, *Amazing Stories* 15.iii (March 1941), 96–113. Re-written as 'Meteor' for August Derleth, ed. *Beachheads in Space* (New York: Pellegrini and Cudahy, 1952), 205–220. Collected in A9.

'The Living Lies', by JB, *New Worlds* 1.ii (October 1946), 2–20, in A30.

'Jizzle', by JB, *Collier's* 123 (8 January 1949), 10–11, 60. Collected in A7, A10.

'Technical Slip', by JBH, *The Arkham Sampler* 2.ii (Spring 1949), 34–45. Collected in A7.

'Adaptation', by JB, *Astounding Science Fiction* 43.v (July 1949), 144–160. In A21.

'Time to Rest', by JBH, *The Arkham Sampler* 2.i (Winter 1949), 55–68; by JB *New Worlds* 2.v (September 1949), 82–92. Collected in A9.

'The Eternal Eve', *Amazing Stories* 24. ix (September 1950), 114–133. In A30.

'The Red Stuff', by JB, *Marvel Science Stories* 3.ii (February 1951), 71–85, 90. Collected in A22.

'No Place Like Earth', by JB, *New Worlds* 3.ix (Spring 1951), 64–83, headed as 'the sequel to "Time to Rest".' As 'Tyrant & Slave-Girl on Planet Venus' in *10 Story Fantasy* 1.i (1951). Title story in John Carnell, ed. *No Place Like Earth* (London: T.V. Boardman, 1952), 13–58. Collected in A23, A27.

'And the Walls Came Tumbling Down...', *Startling Stories* 23.ii (May 1951), 67–77. Collected in A22.

'Bargain from Brunswick', *The Magazine of Fantasy and Science Fiction* 2.iii (June 1951), 22–32. Collected as 'A Present from Brunswick' in A7 and A10.

'Pawley's Peepholes', in *Suspense: The High Tension Magazine* (as 'Operation Peep') 1.ii (Summer 1951), 12–14; *Science-Fantasy* 1.iii (Winter 1951–1952), 2–19; as 'A New Kind of Pink Elephant', *Argosy* 15 (August 1954), 57–73. Collected in A9, A22, A30.

'Pillar to Post', *Galaxy Science Fiction* 3.iii (December 1951), 130–159. Collected in A9. Also published as 'Body and Soul'.

'The Wheel', *Startling Stories* 24.iii (January 1952), 115–120. Collected in A7, A10, A30.

'Survival', *Thrilling Wonder Stories* 39.iii (February 1952), 102–117. In Carnell, ed., *No Place Like Earth*. Collected in A9, A30.

BIBLIOGRAPHY

'Esmeralda', *Magpie* 2.ii (May 1952), 115–128. Collected in A7.

'Affair of the Heart', *Magpie* 2.iv (July 1952), 47–54. Collected in A7.

'Dumb Martian', *Galaxy Science Fiction* 4.iv (July 1952), 49–74. In Edmund Crispen, ed. *Best SF* (London: Faber & Faber, 1955), 56–84. Collected in A9 and A22.

'Time Stops Today', *Future Science Fiction* 3.v (January 1953), 12–25. Collected in A27. Also published as 'Time Out'.

'Close Behind Him', *Fantastic* 2.i (January–February 1953), 113–123, 162. In Tom Boardman, ed. *An ABC of Science Fiction* (London: T.V. Boardman, 1966), 171–183. Collected in A22.

'Chinese Puzzle', *Argosy* 14.ii (February 1953), 5–19, as 'A Stray from Cathay'. Collected in A7, A10, A30.

'The Chronoclasm', *Star Science Fiction Stories*, ed., Frederik Pohl (New York: Ballantine, 1953), 69–90. Collected as 'Chronoplasm' in A9.

'Reservation Deferred', *Fantastic Stories of Imagination* 2.iii (May–June 1953), 28–33. Collected in A7.

'More Spinned Against', *Fantasy Fiction* 1.ii (June 1953), 145–156. Collected in A7 and A10.

'Perforce to Dream', *Woman's Journal* (July 1953), 14, 91–92, 95. Collected in A7, A30.

'Confidence Trick', *Fantastic* 2.iv (July–August 1953), 4–19, 162. Collected in A7 and A10.

'How Do I Do?' *Beyond Fantasy Fiction* 1.ii (September 1953), 99–112; as 'This Year, Next Year', *Woman's Journal* (March 1954), 26–27, 73–74, 77–78. Collected in A7.

'Heaven Scent', *Everybody's Weekly* (10 January 1954), 26–27, 37. Collected in A7 and A10.

'Never on Mars', *Fantastic Universe* 1.iv (January 1954), 62–80. Collected in A30.

'Opposite Numbers', *New Worlds* 8 no.22 (April 1954), 56–69. Collected as 'Opposite Number' in A9 and A10.

'Compassion Circuit', *Fantastic Universe* 2.v (December 1954), 90–98. Collected in A9, A10, A30.

'Wild Flower', *Fantastic Universe* 4.iv (November 1955), 121–122. Collected in A9 and A10.

'Consider Her Ways', *Sometime Never: Three Tales of Imagination*, ed. Maurice Temple Smith (London: Eyre & Spottiswood, 1956), 81–154. Collected in A15.

'But a Kind of Ghost', *Tales of the Frightened* 1.i (Spring 1957), 101–115. Collected in A27.

'For All the Night', *New Worlds* 24 no. 70 (April 1958), 4–31. As 'The Troons of Space: The Space Station A.D. 1994', *Fantastic 7* (November 1958): 8–37. Retitled 'The Space-Station: A.D. 1994' in A13.

BIBLIOGRAPHY

'Idiot's Delight', *New Worlds* 24 no. 72 (June 1958), 4–39. As 'The Troons of Space: The Moon A.D. 2044', *Fantastic* 7 (December 1958): 80–121. Retitled 'The Moon: A.D. 2044' in A13.

'The Thin Gnat-Voices', *New Worlds* 25 no. 73 (July 1958), 85–112. As 'The Troons of Space: Mars A.D. 2094', *Fantastic* 8 (January 1959): 45–74. Retitled 'Mars: A.D. 2094' in A13.

'Space is a Province of Brazil', *New Worlds* 25 no.75 (September 1958), 94–123. As 'The Troons of Space: Venus A.D. 2144', *Fantastic* 8 (February 1959): 96–125. Retitled 'Venus: A.D. 2144' in A13.

'The Killer on the Hill', *Argosy* (US) 347 (October 1958), 50–51, 88. Also published as 'The Meddler'.

'Brief to Counsel', *Argosy* (UK) 20 (February 1959), 28–30. Collected in A30.

'A Long Spoon', *Suspense* (UK) 3 (September 1960), 70–82. Collected in A27.

'The Emptiness of Space', *New Worlds* 34 no. 1000 (November 1960), 38–53. As 'The Asteroids, 2194', *Amazing Stories* 35 (January 1961), 8–23. Collected in A22. Retitled 'The Emptiness of Space: The Asteroids A.D. 2194' in A11, A30.

'A Stitch in Time', *Argosy* (UK) 22 (March 1961), 64–76. Collected in A30.

'It's a Wise Child', *Argosy* (UK) 23 (November 1962), 7–18. Also published as 'Wise Child'.

'Chocky', *Amazing Stories* 37. iii (March 1963), 35–72. Revised as A15.

'In Outer Space There Shone a Star', *TV Times* Christmas Extra (December 1965), 6–8. 58–59.

'A Life Postponed', *Galaxy Science Fiction* 27.v (December 1968), 114–136.

REVIEWS, ESSAYS AND INTERVIEWS

Walter Gillings, 'He's Converting the Masses – John Beynon (Harris) Interviewed', *Scientifiction* 1.i (January 1937), 6–7, 10.

'Revolt of the Animals' by JBH, (Review of Karel Capek's *War with the Newts* and J.S. Bradford's *Even a Worm*), *Scientifiction* 1.ii (April 1937), 8–9.

'Why This Cosmic Wild West Stuff?' by JBH, *Scientifiction* 1.ii (April 1937), 11–12.

'Star Maker is Life's Life-Story', by JBH (Review of Olaf Stapledon), *Scientifiction* 1.ii (June 1937), 12–13.

'The Wonder of Weinbaum', by JBH (Review of Stanley G. Weinbaum's *Dawn of Flame*), *Scientifiction* 1.iv (August 1937), 11.

'Sowing New Thoughts,' *Tales of Wonder* 7 (Summer 1939), 124–125.

'Slave to the Fantastic', by JB (Review of William Hope Hodgson's *The House on the Borderland*), *Fantasy Review* 1.i (February-March 1947), 10.

BIBLIOGRAPHY

'Did Mr. Baker Lose His Way?' by JB (Review of Frank Baker's *Before I Go Hence*), *Fantasy Review* 1.ii (April-May 1947), 14.

'The Fate of the First Men', by JB (Review of Olaf Stapledon's *The Flames*), *Fantasy Review* 1.v (October-November 1947), 12.

'Satirical Salad', by JB (Review of Garnett Radcliffe's *The Lady from Venus*), *Fantasy Review* 1.v (October-November 1947), 14.

'...And Other Expositions', by JB (Review of Gerald Heard's *The Great Fog*), *Fantasy Review* 2.vii (February-March 1948), 13.

'The Flame That Went Out', by JB (Review of Stanley G. Weinbaum's *The Black Flame*), *Fantasy Review* 2.vii (June-July 1948), 8–9.

'Why Blame Wells?' by JB, *Fantasy Review* 2.xii (December 1948–January 1949), 14–15.

'The Incomplete Machen', by JB (Review of Arthur Machen's *Tales of Horror and the Supernatural*), *Fantasy Review* 2.xii (December 1948–January 1949), 23–24.

'And the Green Grass Grew...', by JB (Review of Ward Moore's *Greener Than You Think*), *Fantasy Review* 3.xv (Summer 1949), 21–22.

'Doomsday in Moronia', by JB (Review of Max Ehrlich's *The Big Eye*), *Fantasy Review* 4.xviii (Spring 1950), 30–31.

'Will this hasten the death of the detective thriller?' by JW, *W. H. Smith & Sons Trade Circular* (11 August 1951), 21, 27.

'Not So Simple', by JB, *Authentic Science Fiction Monthly* 1 no. 30 (February 1953), 30–31.

'The Pattern of Science Fiction', by JW, *Science-Fantasy* 3.vii (Spring 1954), 2–4.

'Roar of Rockets!' *John O'London's Weekly* 63 (2 April 1954), 333–334; and in Andy Sawyer, ed. *Science Fiction: Critical Concepts in Media and Cultural Studies* (London and New York: Routledge, 2021), Vol. 1, 190–193.

'Introduction', *The Best from 'New Worlds' Science Fiction*, ed. E. J. Carnell (London: Boardman, 1955), 7–12.

'Science-Fiction: Space-Opera', *The Preparatory School Review* (October 1955), 6–11. Appendix.

'Beginning of the End', (Review of R. C. Churchill's *A Short History of the Future*), *Truth* 155 (7 October 1955), 1248–1249.

'Foreword', *The Seeds of Time* (London: Michael Joseph, 1956), 7–9.

Keith Waterhouse, 'The Master of the Bug-Eyed Monsters', *Daily Mirror* (1 February 1957), 9.

'No Science Fiction This', (Review of Nevil Shute's *On the Beach*), *Smith's Trade News* 1765 (21 September 1957), 36–37.

Elizabeth Hickson, 'Into Outer Space Go the Bug-Eyed Monsters' (with Fred Hoyle, C. S. Lewis et al.), *Sunday Dispatch* (2 March 1958), 6.

'The Scientific Novel', *The Author* 68 (Summer 1958), 90.

BIBLIOGRAPHY

'Science Fiction', (Review of Mordecai Roshwald's *Level 7*, Pat Frank's *Alas, Babylon!*, John Brunner's *The Brink*, and James Blish's *The Canopy of Time*), *The Listener* 62 (3 December 1959), 999, 1001.

Derek Hart, 'Tonight' (interview) BBC TV (6 September 1960), at https://www.bbc.co.uk/archive/tonight--john-wyndham/z7368xs/.

'John Wyndham on Science Fiction: Props for Comment', (Review of Kingsley Amis's *New Maps of Hell*), *John O'London's*y 5 (16 February 1961), 173.

'Cheers to the Triffids' (interview) *Argosy* 22 (March 1961), 3–4.

'John Wyndham on Science Fiction: Verne Revisited', *John O'London's* 5 (6 July 1961), 13.

'Monsters may be real!' *Sunday Pictorial* 2455 (14 January–6 May 1962), 8–9.

'Science Fiction: The Facts', *TV Times* 347 (22 July 1962), 11.

Wilfred De-Ath, 'The Realm of Perhaps' (with Brian Aldiss, Kingsley Amis et al.), *BBC Home Service* (18 March 1963).

'Introduction', *The Secret People*, revised ed. (New York: Lancer Books, 1964), 5–6.

'Personally Speaking', *News of the World* (16 September 1966), 11.

Robert Gunny, 'Home This Afternoon' (discussion about H. G. Wells), BBC Home Service (19 September 1966).

'Pooter' [Alex Hamilton], 'Talking to John Wyndham', *The Times Saturday Review* (16 March 1968), 23.

'Has Science Fiction a Future?' *Radio Times* 182 (30 January 1969), 27–28.

MAIN ADAPTATIONS INTO OTHER MEDIA

Village of the Damned [*The Midwich Cuckoos*], Dir. Wolf Rilla, MGM, 1960.

'The Long Spoon', in 'Storyboard', BBC TV, 1961.

'Jizzle', adapted by John Collier as 'Maria', in 'Alfred Hitchcock Presents', NBC, 1961.

'Dumb Martian', in 'Out of This World', ITV, 1962.

The Day of the Triffids, Dir. Steve Sekely and Freddie Francis, British Security Pictures, 1963.

'Time to Rest', as 'No Place Like Earth', in 'Out of the Unknown', BBC2, 1965.

'Consider Her Ways, in 'Alfred Hitchcock Hour', ITV, 1966.

'Compassion Circuit', CBC, 1966.

'Random Quest', in 'Out of the Unknown', BBC2, 1969.

Quest for Love ['Random Quest'], Dir. Ralph Thomas, Peter Rogers Productions, 1971.

'More Spinned Against', in 'Spine Chillers', BBC1, 1980.

BIBLIOGRAPHY

The Day of the Triffids, 6 episodes, Dir. Ken Hannon, BBC1, 1981.
Chocky, 6 episodes, Dir. Vick Hughes, Thames TV, 1984; Nickelodeon (USA), 1985, etc.
Chocky's Children, 6 episodes, Dir. Vick Hughes, Thames TV, 1985.
Chocky's Challenge, 6 episodes, Dir. Vick Hughes, Thames TV, 1986.
Village of the Damned [*The Midwich Cuckoos*]. Dir. John Carpenter, Alphaville Films, 1995.
'Random Quest', Dir. Luke Watson, BBC4, 2006.
The Day of the Triffids, 2-part, Dir. Nick Copus, BBC1, 2009.
John Wyndham: BBC Radio Drama Collection. Audio CD (London: BBC, 2010).
The Midwich Cuckoos, 7 episodes, Sky Max, 2022.
The Kraken Wakes, Game adaptation, Charisma, 2022.
The Day of the Triffids, TV series, Dir. Johan Renck, Angry Films, 2025?

CRITICAL MATERIAL

Adams, Alexander, 'John Wyndham, Genius and Prophet', *Brazen Head* (3 June 2022), https://brazen-head.org/2022/06/03/john-wyndham-genius-and-prophet/.
Adamson, Joni and Catriona Sandilands, 'Insinuations: Thinking Plant Politics with *The Day of the Triffids*', in Monica Gagliano, John C. Ryan and Patrícia Vieira (eds), *The Language of Plants: Science, Philosophy, Literature* (Minneapolis and London: University of Minnesota Press, 2017), 234–252.
Alaimo, Stacy, 'Deep Sea Speculations: Science and the Animating Arts of William Beebe, Else Bostelmann, and John Wyndham', *Journal of the Fantastic in the Arts* 33.iii (September 2022), 69–91.
Aldiss, Brian W., 'John Wyndham Parkes Lucas Beynon Harris (John Wyndham', *Dictionary of National Biography 1961–1970* (Oxford: Oxford University Press, 1981), 491–493.
Aldiss, Brian W. and David Wingrove, *Trillion Year Spree* (London: Gollancz, 1986), 252–255.
Amis, Kingsley, *New Maps of Hell. A Survey of Science Fiction* (London: Victor Gollancz, 1961).
Andrews, Stephen E., 'John Wyndham's "Obscure" Works – Science Fiction and Crime', *Outlaw Bookseller* n.d. https://www.youtube.com/watch?v=zAnwBOpcHXY.
Anon. 'An Introduction to John Wyndham,' *Children's Literature Review* 190 (2014), 161–204.
Ashley, Mike, *The Time Machines: The Story of the Science-Fiction Pulp Magazines from the Beginning to 1950* (Liverpool: Liverpool University Press, 2000).

BIBLIOGRAPHY

—, *Transformations: The Story of the Science Fiction Magazines from 1950 to 1970* (Liverpool: Liverpool University Press, 2005).

Atwood, Margaret, 'Chocky, the Kindly Body Snatcher', 'Afterword'. *Chocky* (New York: NYRB, 2015), https://slate.com/culture/2015/09/margaret-atwood-chocky-the-kindly-alien-invader-in-john-wyndhams-last-book.html/.

Baxter, John, 'Plant Power', *Radio Times* 232 (September 1981), 76–78.

—, 'The Making of BBC's *Day of the Triffids*', *Starburst* 4 (1 March 2002): 28–35.

BBC, *John Wyndham: A BBC Radio Drama Collection* (London: BBC, 2017) (adaptations).

Bedore, Pamela, 'John Wyndham: The Real Pioneer in Science Fiction', *WondriumDaily* (30 May 2021), https://www.wondriumdaily.com/john-wyndham-the-real-pioneer-in-science-fiction/.

—, 'The Post-Apocalyptic Dystopia in *The Chrysalids*', *WondriumDaily* (31 May 2021), https://www.wondriumdaily.com/the-post-apocalyptic-dystopia-in-the-chrysalids/.

Binns, Amy, *Hidden Wyndham. Life, Love, Letters* (London: Grace Judson Press, 2019).

Bleiler, E. F., 'Luncheon with John Wyndham', *Extrapolation* 25.v (Winter 1984), 314–317.

Boluk, Stephanie and Wylie Lenz (eds), *Generation Zombie: Essays on the Living Dead in Modern Culture* (Jefferson NC and London: McFarland, 2011).

Bruhm, Steven, 'The Global Village of the Damned: A Counter-Narrative for the Post-War Child', *Narrative* 24.ii (2016), 156–173.

Bueno, Claire, 'Aisling Loftus: The Midwich Cuckoos Interview', *Premiere Scene* (June 14, 2022), https://premierescene.net/2022/06/14/aisling-loftus-the-midwich-cuckoos-interview/.

Calmgrove, 'Each One in Its Humour', *Wyrd & Wonder* (31 May 2021), https://calmgrove.wordpress.com/2021/05/31/jizzle/.

Carnell, John, 'No Comparison...' *New Worlds Fiction of the Future* 2.6 (Spring 1950), 37.

—, 'Phases of S-f', *New Worlds Science Fiction* 23.69 (March 1958), 2–3.

Cheng, John, *Astounding Wonder: Imagining Science and Science Fiction in Interwar America* (Philadelphia: University of Pennsylvania Press, 2012).

Clareson, Thomas D. and Alice S. Clareson, 'The Neglected Fiction of John Wyndham: "Consider Her Ways", *Trouble with Lichen* and *Web*', in Rhys Garnett and R.J. Ellis (eds), *Science Fiction Roots and Branches: Contemporary Critical Approaches* (London: Palgrave Macmillan, 1990), 88–103.

BIBLIOGRAPHY

Clute, John, 'John Wyndham', in John Clute and David Langford, eds. *SFE: The Encyclopedia of Science Fiction*. 4th ed. 2021, https://sf-encyclopedia.com/.

Colebatch, Hal G. P., 'Ethics in Science-Fiction Disasters,' *Quadrant* 51.iii (2007), 72–76.

Conefrey, Mick, dir. *John Wyndham: The Invisible Man of Science Fiction* (BBC TV Documentary, 2005), https://www.youtube.com/watch?v=K9WPP-5jemA.

Downey, Adrian M., 'Critical Posthumanism, *The Chrysalids*, and Educational Change', *Changing English* 30.i (2023), 66–76.

Elsom, John, 'John Wyndham', in John Wakeman, ed. *World Authors 1950–1970* (New York: H. W. Wilson, 1975), 1573–1574.

Falkner, J. S., 'Interrogating 20th Century British Narratives of Progress in *The Day of the Triffids* and *The Death of Grass*' (2017), https://www.academia.edu/33082450/Interrogating_20th_Century_British_Narratives_of_Progress_in_The_Day_of_The_Triffids_and_The_Death_of_Grass.

Flood, Leslie, 'Introduction', *The Best of John Wyndham, 1932–1949* (London: Sphere, 1973), 7–11; and *The Best of John Wyndham, 1951–1960* (London: Sphere, 1977), 6–10.

Folk, Kate, 'Introduction', *Trouble with Lichen* (New York: Modern Library, 2022).

Gillings, Walter, 'The Writer People Believed In'. *Cosmos: Science Fantasy Review* 2 (May 1969).

—, 'Before the Triffids ...', *Wanderers of Time* (London: Coronet, 1973), 7–8.

—, 'The Fate of the Martians', *Sleepers of Mars* (London: Coronet, 1973), 7–8.

—, 'Modern Masters of Science Fiction 3: John Wyndham', *Science Fiction Monthly* 1.ix (1974), 8–9.

Gochenour, Phil, '"Different Conditions Set Different Standards:" The Ecology of Ethics in John Wyndham's *The Day of the Triffids*', *The New York Review of Science Fiction* 23.x (June 2011), http://www.nyrsf.com/2011/06/index.html/.

Griffiths, C. M., 'A Note on The Day of the Triffids and its Film Adaptations', https://www.academia.edu/7492411/A_note_on_The_Day_of_the_Triffids_and_its_film_adaptations.

Hansen, Solveig Lena, 'Otherness, Cloning, and Morality in John Wyndham's *The Midwich Cuckoos* (1957)', *Journal of Medical Humanities* 43 (2022), 547–560.

Harpold, Terry, 'The End Begins: John Wyndham's Zombie Cozy', in Stephanie Boluk and Wylie Lenz (eds), *Generation Zombie: Essays on the Living Dead in Modern Culture* (Jefferson NC: McFarland, 2011), 156–164.

BIBLIOGRAPHY

Harris, Vivian Beynon, '[My Brother,] John Wyndham, 1903–1969', ed. David Ketterer, *Foundation: The International Review of Science Fiction*, 75 (Spring 1999), 18–50.

Harrison, M. John, 'Introduction', *The Chrysalids* (London: Penguin, 2000), i–xi.

Heathcote, Christopher, 'Triffids, Daleks and the Fragility of Civilisation', *Quadrant* (1 November 2014), 80–88.

Hubble, Nick, 'Five English Disaster Novels, 1951–1972', *Foundation* 95.iii (2005), 89–103.

Hurst, L. J., '"We Are the Dead": A Commentary on *The Day of the Triffids* and *Nineteen Eighty-Four*', *Vector* 133 (August–September 1986), 4–5, https://web.archive.org/web/20130810155228/http://dspace.dial.pipex.com/l.j.hurst/weredead.htm.

—, 'Remembrance of Things to Come? *Nineteen Eighty-Four* and *The Day of the Triffids* Again', *Vector* 201 (September–October 1986), 15–17.

James, Edward, 'John Wyndham', in James Gunn (ed.), *The New Encyclopedia of Science Fiction* (New York: Viking, 1988), 515–516.

Kagarlitsky, Julius, 'John Wyndham', in Noelle Watson and Paul E. Schellinger (eds), *Twentieth-Century Science Fiction Writers* (London: St. James Press, 1991), 892–893.

Kelly, Melanie, *A Guide to 'The Day of the Triffids'* (Bristol: The Great Reading Adventure, 2004), https://www.bristolideas.co.uk/wp-content/uploads/2021/03/GRA-2004-Readers-Guide.pdf.

Kerslake, Patricia, *Science Fiction and Empire* (Liverpool: Liverpool University Press, 2007).

Ketterer, David, 'John Wyndham and the "Searing Anguishes of Childhood": From "Fairy Story" to *Chocky*', *Extrapolation* 41.ii (2000), 87–103.

—, 'A Part of the … Family[?]: John Wyndham's *The Midwich Cuckoos* as Estranged Autobiography', in Patrick Parrinder (ed.), *Learning from Other Worlds: Estrangement, Cognition, and the Politics of Science Fiction and Utopia* (Liverpool: Liverpool University Press, 2000), 146–177.

—, '"Vivisection": Schoolboy "John Wyndham's" First Publication?', *Science Fiction Studies* 26.ii (July 1999), 303–311; expanded in *Foundation: The International Review of Science Fiction* 29 (Summer 2000), 70–83.

—, 'The Genesis of the Triffids', *The New York Review of Science Fiction* 16.vii (March 2004), 11–14.

—, 'Questions and Answers: The Life and Fiction of John Wyndham', *The New York Review of Science Fiction* 16.vii (March 2004), 1, 6–10.

—, 'John Wyndham: The Facts of Life Sextet', in David Seed (ed.), *A Companion to Science Fiction* (Oxford: Blackwell, 2005), 375–388.

—, 'John Wyndham and the Sins of His Father: Damaging Disclosures in Court', *Extrapolation* 46.ii (Summer 2005), 163–188.

—, 'John Wyndham (1903[?]–1969)', in Kerry Miner and Jenni Ramoned (eds), *The Literary Encyclopedia* Volume 1.2.1.09: *English Writing and Culture: Postwar and Contemporary Britain , 1945– Present* (7 November 2006), https://www.litencyc.com/php/speople.php?rec=true&UID=4820/.

—, 'Race in SF and John Wyndham's Colour-Schemed Future', *Science Fiction Studies* 34.iii (2007), 527–529.

—, '"None of the Old Isms": A Major Deletion in *The Day of the Triffids*", *Foundation: The International Review of Science Fiction* 36? (Winter 2007), 8–9.

—, 'John Wyndham's *Chocky* (1968): The First Covert Alternate World?', *Science Fiction Studies* 35.ii (July 2008), 352–355.

—, 'PLAN FOR CHAOS/FURY OF CREATION: An Unpublished Science-Fiction Thriller by John Beynon/John Lucas (aka John Wyndham)', *Foundation: The International Review of Science Fiction* 74 (Autumn 1998), 8–25. Revised and extended as 'Introduction: A Ground-Breaking Cloned Nazis Thriller' to John Wyndham, *Plan for Chaos*, eds David Ketterer and Andy Sawyer (Liverpool: Liverpool University Press, 2009), 1–27.

—, 'The Corrected and Expanded Introduction to *Plan for Chaos* by John Wyndham', *HUBbub* (17 November 2009), http://sfhubbub.blogspot.com/2009/11/revised-and-updated-introduction-to.html.

—, 'The Case for Rape: John Wyndham and Octavia Butler', *Science Fiction Studies* 38.ii (July 2011), 373–376.

—, 'John Wyndham's World War III and his Abandoned *Fury of Creation* Trilogy', in David Seed (ed.), *Future Wars: The Anticipations and the Fears* (Liverpool: Liverpool University Press, 2012), 103–129.

—, 'When and Where Was John Wyndham Born?', *Foundation: The International Review of Science Fiction* 42 (Summer 2012/13), 22–39.

—, 'Who Originated the SF Term "Chronoclasm"?', *Science Fiction Studies* 40.i (March 2013), 199–200.

—, 'John Wyndham's Martian Rover as Illustrated by "Chester"', *Science Fiction Studies* 41.iii (November 2014), 694–695.

—, 'John B. Harris's Mars Rover on Earth', *Science Fiction Studies* 41.ii (July 2014), 474–475.

—, 'John Wyndham's "The Living Lies" in Ray Palmer's *Other Worlds*', *Science Fiction Studies* 41.ii (July 2014), 473–474.

—, 'Howell Davies and John Wyndham', *Science Fiction Studies* 42.ii (July 2015), 405–408.

—, 'Triffid Alley'. *Science Fiction Studies* 42.iii (November 2015), 613.

—, 'Flag Flying Aspidistras and Triffids: John Beynon Harris and Eric Blair Meet', *Science Fiction Studies* 43.iii (November 2016), 612–615.

—, 'The Complete *Midwich Cuckoos', Foundation* 46.i (2017), 47–60.

—, 'Note on "The Complete *Midwich Cuckoos"', Foundation: The International Review of Science Fiction* 46.ii (2017), 72–73.

Kirby, David A., 'The Threat of Materialism in the Age of Genetics: DNA at the Drive-In', in Gary D. Rhodes (ed.), *Horror at the Drive-In: Essays in Popular Americana* (Jefferson NC: McFarland, 2008), 241–258.

Kleeman, Alexandra, 'Introduction', *The Kraken Wakes* (New York: Modern Library, 2022), ix–xii.

Krome, Frederic, Gregory Loving and C. Phoebe Reeves, 'The Concept of the Human in John Wyndham's *The Chrysalids*: Political Imagery, Female Agency and Theistic Evolution', *Interdisciplinary Humanities* 32.ii (Summer 2015), 52–64.

Langford, Barry, 'Introduction', *The Day of the Triffids* (London: Penguin, 1999), vii–xvii.

LaRose, Nicole, 'Zombies in a "Deep, Dark Ocean of History": Danny Boyle's Infected and John Wyndham's Triffids as Metaphors of Postwar Britain', in Stephanie Boluk and Wylie Lenz (eds), *Generation Zombie: Essays on the Living Dead in Modern Culture* (Jefferson NC: McFarland, 2011), 165–181.

Latham, Rob, 'The New Wave "Revolution," 1960–76', in Roger Luckhurst (ed.), *Science Fiction: A Literary History* (London: British Library, 2017), 157–180.

Lawler, Donald L., 'Wyndham, *The Day of the Triffids*', in Frank N. Magill (ed.), *Survey of Science Fiction Literature* (Englewood Cliffs NJ: Sale Press, 1979), Vol. I, 502–507.

Lerner, Laurence, 'Novels about the Future', *The Listener* 68 (26 July 1962), 143–144.

Link, Kelly, 'Introduction', *The Midwich Cuckoos* (New York: Modern Library, 2022), https://gizmodo.com/midwich-cuckoos-rerelease-john-wyndham-kelly-link-1848800024.

Link, Miles, '"A Very Primitive Matter": John Wyndham on Catastrophe and Survival', *The Irish Journal of Gothic and Horror Studies* 14 (Summer 2015), 63–80.

Liptak, Andrew, 'John Wyndham and the Global Expansion of Science Fiction', *Kirkus* (17 May 2015), https://www.kirkusreviews.com/news-and-features/articles/john-wyndham-and-global-expansion-science-fiction/.

Luckhurst, Roger, *Science Fiction* (Cambridge: Polity Press, 2005).

Maatta, Jerry, 'The Politics of Post-Apocalypse: Ideologies on Trial in John Wyndham's *The Day of the Triffids*', in Christian Baron, Peter Nicolai Halvorsen and Christine Cornea (eds), *Science Fiction, Ethics and the Human Condition* (New York: Springer, 2017), 207–226.

BIBLIOGRAPHY

—, '"Bloody Unnatural Brutes": Anthropomorphism, Colonialism and the Return of the Repressed John Wyndham's *The Day of the Triffids*', in Katherine E. Bishop, David Higgins and Jerry Määttä (eds), *Speculative Vegetation: Plants in Science Fiction* (Cardiff: University of Wales Press, 2020), 32–55.

Macdonald, Kate, 'John Wyndham's Trouble with Lichen' (2015), https://katemacdonald.net/2015/03/30/john-wyndhams-trouble-with-lichen/.

Manlove, C. N., 'Everything Slipping Away: John Wyndham's *The Day of the Triffids*', *Journal of the Fantastic in the Arts* 4.i (1991), 29–53.

Matthews, Graham J., 'What We Think About When We Think About Triffids: The Monstrous Vegetal in Post-war British Science Fiction', in Dawn Keetley and Angela Tenga (eds), *Plant Horror: Approaches to the Monstrous Vegetal in Fiction and Film* (London: Palgrave Macmillan, 2016), 111–127.

Maxwell, J. G., 'The Why of Wyndham', *Australian Science Fiction Review* 12 (October 1967), 20–21.

McKay, Anthony, 'Beware the Stare … That Will Paralyse the World! The Making of *Village of the Damned*', *Little Shoppe of Horrors: The Journal of Classic British Horror Films* 42 (May 2019), 15–75.

—, 'Beware the Eyes that Paralyse! They Come to Conquer the World! The Making of *Children of the Damned*', *The Little Shoppe of Horrors: The Journal of Classic British Horror Films*, 43 (October 2019), 31–66.

McViety, Jon, et al. 'The Day of the Triffids?' *Emergency Medicine Journal* 27 (2010–11), 883–884.

Michel, Lincoln, 'Introduction', *Stowaway to Mars* (New York: Modern Library, 2022), ix–xiii.

Miller, T. S., 'Lives of the Monster Plants: The Revenge of the Vegetable in the Age of Animal Studies', *Journal of the Fantastic in the Arts* 23.iii (2012), 460–479.

Moore, Matthew, 'Utopian Ambivalences in Wyndham's *Web*', *Foundation* 32 (Autumn 2003), 47–56.

Morgart, James, 'Deleuzions of Ecohorror: Weighing Al Gore's Ecostrategy Against *The Day of the Triffids*', *Horror Studies* 8.i (2017), 115–130.

Moskowitz, Sam, 'SF Profile: John Wyndham', *Amazing Stories* 38.vi (June 1964), 29–40; collected as 'John Wyndham', in *Seekers of Tomorrow: Masters of Modern Science Fiction* (Westport CT: Hyperion Press, 1974), 118–132.

Oliver-Hobley, Christie, '"All et by the cannible savidges": Decolonization, Heteroglossia and the Nuclear/Unclear Spiders in John Wyndham's *Web*', *Foundation: The International Review of Science Fiction* 51 (2022), 63–77.

BIBLIOGRAPHY

Owen, David, 'John Wyndham and His 1950s Apocalyptic Novels: Bad News for the Hoi Polloi', in David Owen and Cristina Phidon (eds), *The Spectre of Defeat in Post-War British and US Literature: Experience, Memory and Post-Memory* (Newcastle upon Tyne: Cambridge Scholars, 2021), 2–10.

Pollard, Neil, 'Early Triffids', *Docplayer* (2017), https://docplayer. net/138331565-Early-triffids-by-neil-pollard.html.

—, 'The Very Un-Cosy Catastrophe: John Wyndham's Original Ending to *The Kraken Wakes*', *Triffid Alley* (2018), https://docplayer. net/118170054-The-very-un-cosy-catastrophe-john-wyndham-s-original-ending-to-the-kraken-wakes.html/.

—, 'The Early Edition of *The Day of the Triffids* that is not so Early', *Triffid Alley* (11 August 2020), http://triffidalley.com/ta_research/tdot_not_1951.pdf/.

Priest, Christopher, 'John Wyndham and H. G. Wells', *Way Back Machine* (2000), https://web.archive.org/web/20190722220259/https://christopher-priest.co.uk/essays/contemporaries-portrayed/john-wyndham-h-g-wells/.

—, 'Introduction', *The Chrysalids* (New York: NYRB, 2008), vii–xiii.

—, 'The Life Awakes' (28 November 2019) (review of Binns), https://christopher-priest.co.uk/.

Priyadarsini, Preety, 'Redefining Norms: Accepting the "Other" in John Wyndham's *The Chrysalids* and *The Midwich Cuckoos*', *Research Journal of English Language and Literature (RJELAL)* 10.iv (Oct.– Dec. 2022), 1–7.

Pysek, Petr, 'On the Road to Understanding: From John Wyndham to Reality', *Diversity and Distribution* 3.iii (May 2003), 251–252.

Raisborough, Jayne and Susan Watkins, 'Critical Future Studies and Age: Attending to Future Imaginings of Age and Ageing', *Culture Unbound* 13.ii (2021), 15–37.

Rebellato, Dan, 'John Wyndham: No Place Like Earth' *BBC Radio 4* (24 December 2005), http://www.danrebellato.co.uk/john-wyndham-documentary/.

—, 'John Wyndham: The Unread Bestseller', *The Guardian* (20 December 2010), https://www.theguardian.com/books/booksblog/2010/dec/20/john-wyndham-unread-bestseller/.

— (et al.) 'John Wyndham: The Invisible Man of Science Fiction' (BBC 2005), https://thetvdb.com/series/bbc-documentaries/episodes/4546824/.

Rees, Amanda, 'From Technician's Extravaganza to Logical Fantasy: Science and Society in John Wyndham's Postwar Fiction, 1951–1960', *Osiris* 34.i (October 2019), 277–296.

BIBLIOGRAPHY

Reichard, S. H. and Peter White, 'Horticulture as a Pathway of Invasive Plant Introductions in the United States,' *Bioscience* 51.ii (2001), 103–113.

Roberts, Adam, 'Introduction', *The Wyndham Collection: The Day of the Triffids* (ix–xiii), *The Midwich Cuckoos* (ix–xiii), *The Chrysalids* (vii–xii), 3 vols. (London: Folio Society, 2010).

Ruddick, Nicholas, *Ultimate Island: On the Nature of British Science Fiction* (Westport CT: Greenwood Press, 1993).

Sahin, Ferit, 'From the Cocoon into a Butterfly: Wyndham's Theocratic Dystopia as a Bildungsroman', *RumeliDE Journal of Language and Literature Studies* 31 (2022), 1462–1473.

Sawyer, Andy, 'On Speller on Wyndham', *Banana Wings* 12 (1998), 38–40.

—, 'The Wyndham Archives and "The Return of the Triffids"', *Foundation* 74 (Autumn 1998), 3–7.

—, 'A Stiff Upper Lip, and a Trembling Lower One: John Wyndham on Screen', in I. Q. Hunter (ed.), *British Science Fiction Cinema* (London: Routledge, 1999), 75–87.

—, 'John Wyndham and the Fantastic', *Wormwood* 3 (2004), 51–62.

—, 'Midwich Abandoned: An Unpublished "Sequel" by John Wyndham or: "It Comes of Being a Hybrid', *Foundation* 35 (2005), 7–17.

Scarborough, John, 'John Wyndham, 1903–1969', in E. F. Bleiler (ed.), *Science Fiction Writers: Critical Studies of the Major Authors from the Early Nineteenth Century to the Present Day* (New York: Scribner's, 1982), 219–224.

Seidel, Matthew James, 'The First Climate Fiction Masterpiece: On John Wyndham's *The Kraken Wakes*', *LA Review of Books* (15 October 2022), https://www.lareviewofbooks.org/article/the-first-climate-fiction-masterpiece-on-john-wyndhams-1953-novel-the-kraken-wakes/.

Simpson, Ian J., 'Wyndham's Cosy Warnings', *Vector,* 199 (May/June 1998), 16–19.

Slattery, Mark, 'Down on the Triffid Farm', *New Statesman* (19 November 2001), 38–40.

Sleight, Graham, 'Yesterday's Tomorrows: John Wyndham', *Locus Magazine* (December 2010), https://locusmag.com/2010/12/graham-sleights-yesterdays-tomorrows-john-wyndham/.

Smith, Denis, '*The Kraken Wakes*: Corporate Social Responsibility and the Political Dynamics of the Hazardous Waste Issue', *Industrial Crisis Quarterly* 5.iii (1991), 189–207.

Speller, Maureen Kincaird, 'Skiffy Stuff', *Banana Wings* 11 (1998), 53–58.

Stableford, Brian, *Scientific Romance in Britain, 1890–1950.* (London: Fourth Estate, 1985).

Stephensen-Payne, Phil, *John Wyndham: Creator of the Cosy Catastrophe: A Working Bibliography,* 3rd ed. (Leeds: Galactic Central Publications, 2001).

BIBLIOGRAPHY

Stock, Adam, 'The Blind Logic of Plants: Enlightenment and Evolution in John Wyndham's *The Day of the Triffids*', *Science Fiction Studies* 42.iii (November 2015), 433–457.

—, 'The Future-As-Past in Dystopian Fiction', *Poetics Today* 37.iii (2016), 415–442.

Stratton, Jon, 'The Triffids: The Sense of Place, Popular Music and Society', *Popular Music and Society* 30.iii (2007), 377–399.

Tearle, Adam, 'Wells's Heir? *The Seeds of Time*', *Dispatches from the Secret Library* (13 January 2019), https://interestingliterature.com/2019/01/wellss-heir-john-wyndhams-the-seeds-of-time-review/. And in *The Secret Library* (London: Michael O'Mara, 2016).

Temple, William F., 'Talking about John Wyndham: Plagiarism in SF', *Australian Science Fiction Review* 12 (October 1967), 16–19.

Thomas, G. W., 'The Early Science Fiction of John Wyndham', *Darkworlds Quarterly* (9 November 2019), https://darkworldsquarterly.gwthomas.org/the-early-science-fiction-of-john-wyndham/.

—, 'John Wyndham's Planet Plane and The Sleepers of Mars', *Darkworlds Quarterly* (25 December 2020), https://darkworldsquarterly.gwthomas.org/john-wyndhams-planet-plane-and-the-sleepers-of-mars/.

—, 'Sam Moskowitz's "Uncrowned Masters" (1940)', *Darkworlds Quarterly* (7 February 2021), https://darkworldsquarterly.gwthomas.org/sam-moskowitzs-uncrowned-masters-1940/.

Tisdall, Laura, 'The Psychologist, the Psychoanalyst and the "Extraordinary Child" in Postwar British Science Fiction', *Medical Humanities* 42.iv (2016), 4–9.

—, '"We Have Come to Be Destroyed": the "Extraordinary" Child in Science Fiction Cinema in Early Cold War Britain', *History of the Social Sciences* 34.v (2021), 8–31.

—, 'The Midwich Cuckoos: What the Latest Remake Tells Us About Our Fears for the Next Generation', *The Conversation* (22 June 2022), https://theconversation.com/the-midwich-cuckoos-what-the-latest-remake-tells-us-about-our-fears-for-the-next-generation-185452.

VanderMeer, Jeff, 'Introduction', *The Day of the Triffids* (New York: Modern Library, 2022), vii–x.

Wagner, Thomas M., 'The Chrysalids, 1955' *SF Reviews* (2004), www.sfreviews.net/chrysalids.html/.

Walton, Jo, 'Who Survives the Cosy Catastrophe?', *Foundation* 34 (Spring 2005), 34–39.

—, 'Telepathy and Tribulation: John Wyndham's *The Chrysalids*', *TOR.com Newsletter* (27 October 2008), https://www.tor.com/2008/10/27/the-chrysalids/.

—, 'A Way the World Ends: John Wyndham's *The Kraken Wakes*', *TOR. com Newsletter* (13 October 2009), https://www.tor.com/2009/10/13/the-way-the-world-ends-john-wyndhams-lemgthe-kraken-wakeslemg/.

Webster, Owen, 'John Wyndham as Novelist of Ideas', *SF Commentary* 44/45 (1975), 39–50.

Wells, H. G., *Seven Famous Novels* (New York: Alfred A. Knopf, 1934).

Wolfe, Gary K., '*The Midwich Cuckoos*', in Frank N. Magill (ed.), *Survey of Science Fiction Literature*, 5 vols. (Englewood Cliffs NJ: Salem Press, 1979), Vol. 3, 1391–1395; and '*Re-Birth*' [*The Chrysalids*], ibid. Vol. 4, 1755–1758.

Wolf-Meyer, Matthew J., *Theory for the World to Come, Speculative Fiction and Apocalyptic Anthropology* (Minneapolis, MN: University of Minneapolis Press, 2019).

Wymer, Rowland, 'How "Safe" is John Wyndham? A Closer Look at his Work, with Particular Reference to *The Chrysalids*', *Foundation: The International Review of Science Fiction* 55 (Summer 1992), 25–36.

Yeates, Robert, 'Gender and Ethnicity in Post-Apocalyptic Suburbia', *Journal of the Fantastic in the Arts* 27.iii (2016), 411–434.

Appendix

'Science-Fiction: Space-Opera'
By John Wyndham

There can be few classes of writing where good currency has suffered more from the pressure of bad than that already handicapped with the lamentable title of 'science-fiction'.

Most categories of popular fiction have developed sub-sections that are fairly easily identified. The distinctions between the detective novel, the problem detective story, the detective thriller, and so on, are not difficult to perceive; nor is that between a genuine love story and a suburban 'romance'; and though *I, Claudius* and *Forever Amber* will both be classified by a bookseller as historical novels, the latter does not leak odium over the former.[1] In science-fiction, however, there has been almost no accretion into recognisable groups, so that all are singed by the flame of the same rocket.

SCIENCE-FICTION DEFINED

Nevertheless, this ill-mapped territory does have three main cantons, each with a number of districts, which all come under the definition recently coined by Mr. Edmund Crispin in his introduction to *Best S-F* (Faber): that the science-fiction story 'presupposes a technology, or an effect of technology, or a disturbance of the natural order, such as humanity, up to the time of writing, has not in actual fact experienced.'[2]

It is a wide and generous definition – rather too wide to assist discrimination, for it is possible to presuppose such matters intelligently, stupidly, carelessly, obsessively, and in innumerable other ways. The evidence of his own collection suggests that he does expect at least an intelligent approach, and, if that is so, he has not only severely qualified his own definition, but also ruled out some 90 per cent of the material which the publishing trade understands to be science-fiction. For the three main categories are these: the 'Scientific Romance', as Wells, with some confessed dissatisfaction in the term, described his application of novel technique to the definition;[3] the science-fiction story proper – that is to say the type of story for which an American editor coined the term – where careful, conscientious deduction and attention to logical probability, as in the work of, say, Isaac Asimov and Arthur Clarke, are the overriding considerations;[4] and, finally, the overwhelming mass of hackwork known as 'space-opera' where any trammelling considerations of science and logic are thrown off, and anything goes so long as it is fast-moving and exciting. In this category, too, come the comic-strips, television serials, and almost every attempt, since THINGS TO COME, to make a science-fiction film.[5]

No literary form ever started at the bottom, and worked up; almost every kind of written rubbish is a degenerate offspring, often bearing so much superficial resemblance to its parents that the sins of the children are visited upon the father. In this case, the similarity of the 'props' used by all three kinds is the more confusing because they are still only semi-familiar to English readers. Moreover, it is not only the 'props' of the first two categories that have been seized by the lower orders; many of their conventions have been taken over, too. This tends both to contaminate the upper categories, and to obscure the fact that the third really has little to do with them, that it is, indeed, just an old friend in disguise: the Western, the exploration-adventure, the pirate-tale, the thriller, given a new packaging and expressed in a new idiom for marketing purposes. As such, it is without significance other than the ability of cheap publishers to work up fashions – and already this particular fashion has recently been suffering a serious reverse among American children under the impact of a trapper character, one Davy Crockett.[6]

APPENDIX

JULES VERNE

This space-farrago did, however, have reputable ancestors, of whom the first was Verne.

Jules Verne was the product of a new age.[7] He could not, fifty years before, have written as he did one hundred years ago. He was set in a growing technology, and the sense of progress through technology was spreading rapidly to create a climate of thought which had never existed before. A readership that was just becoming aware that the world which had hitherto changed almost imperceptibly was now about to pass into a phase of rapid change, hailed him as a prophet – which, indeed, in the common usage of the word, he was.

But he was a prophet who limited his field to technology, and disregarded the effects of its impact on society. More through his individuality than his sagacity he avoided discomforting his readers by suggesting that the structure of their lives would be in any way changed – and fortunately, for the mid-nineteenth century man would have been even more opposed to such a proposition than is the mid-twentieth century man. In doing so, he set a pattern which was closely followed in the form's recrudescence as 'science-fiction' in 1925.[8]

THE AMERICAN APPROACH

It was then, and still is, generally true of American science-fiction that the invention, the gadget, the discovery, the new twist, is its primary consideration. Writing, construction, characterization, all play second-fiddle to novelty of idea, and though this may be deplored, it has to be remembered that this is not the Arts side; it is the Science side, at play. The protagonist and the whole cast of a story set in 2155, or 2555, customarily remain the stock types of 1955. The social systems in which they find themselves, or which they favour, tend to take their shapes from the date at which the story was written – the futures envisaged in the Roosevelt era differ interestingly from those foreseen now that the Republicans are in power. The Russians, who have several times drawn attention to the fascist tone of this kind of fiction, cannot be writers who have ever tried to write it. The effect is largely the outcome of technical writing problems. The author has no room, even if he had the inclination, to deal exhaustively with complex administration. He has to attach his readers' interest to one, or a few, individuals, and in order to avoid diffusing their attention from the main problem he uses simplified circumstances and familiar properties, and then gets down to working out within the rules of probability the effects of his chosen 'disturbance of the natural order' upon the setting.

In doing this he is playing a game with his knowledgeable reader very similar to that which the detective-story writer plays with his reader. In both cases the relative values of such 'props' as spaceships and world dictators, or corpses and poison bottles, are tacitly understood, as, too, are the rules, and each kind of author is working out his problem, while each kind of reader watches him, hawk-eyed for a slip. (Huh! Forgot to warn suspect before questioning him, or, Huh! How do you *pour* out a drink in no-gravity conditions?)

It has to be remembered that science-fiction in America has now a generation of development behind it – time to build up a considerable body of conventions, taboos, and jargon which have become almost necessary if the same introductory ground is not to be covered again and again. Inevitably, this must leave a newcomer somewhat at sea, but it is no good expecting something which has been thirty years agrowing in a different mental climate to be immediately familiar.

A JOURNALIST – A NOVELIST

Verne, then, was a good journalist who was interested in displaying the devices that he found implicit in the new technical progress. Wells, on the other hand, wrote as a novelist interested in the effects of the discoveries upon people. He saw in it, moreover, opportunities for propaganda, satire, and controversy neglected by Verne. He did not break with all accepted standards to elevate novelty above the rest; rather, he took novelty and fitted it into existing patterns, and in doing this he produced a type of work which appealed, and continues to appeal, to a wider stratum of readers than the other.

By and large, the type of story which pleases the more

APPENDIX

specialist readership (the 'fans') in America looks to English eyes ingenious, slick, mechanical, careful in argument, careless in style, and considerably weakened in holding power by lack of attention to the humanities.

THE ENGLISH STORY 'STUFFY'?

By contrast, the average English story (or perhaps one should say European story) tending more towards the Wells pattern, strikes the American enthusiast as stuffy, slow, pointlessly padded out, unadventurous, and, least forgivable of all, old-fashioned in expression.

The enthusiasts on both sides, however, concede one another's national peculiarities and read one another's productions with some toleration because they are at one upon another point of judgement: that the story should have intention – that is to say that the author should have some theory hinging upon one or other of the sciences, and be using the story to put it across. (If he does not have this, he is not writing science-fiction proper; he is in one of the border territories, very probably space-opera.) And also, that he should keep to the rules of the game.

The rules are more difficult to define even than those governing the detective story, yet basically similar since the ethic of both is that the author plays fair with the reader. The kind of rule that simply must not be broken is best shown, perhaps, by example.

WHERE H. G. WELLS FELL DOWN

Mr. Wells' works in general still exact much respect as period pieces of the genre, but there is one certainly that all science-fiction purists are agreed simply *will not do*. They may concede that *The Food of the Gods* is a readable story, and good parable, but it is *not* science-fiction.[9] Their reasons are technical:

Mr Wells postulates a food which enormously stimulates growth – fair enough, now let's see what he does with it, what logical conclusions he draws from its existence. Well, the answer is, he does not: he produces giant wasps, and goes on to giant

151

men. Your science-fiction 'fan' is not going to accept that. He knows that a giant wasp is an impossibility because it could not have enough surface area to supply it with the amount of oxygen its bulk would require. Similarly, he knows that the lungs of a human being would be inadequate, and that its skeleton would collapse from the body's weight long before it reached the height of forty feet. In fact, the author has not played fair. He has deliberately falsified the consequences of his premise; thereby assuming that the reader is either ignorant, or venal; and the whole situation is morally quite indefensible. (Quite as bad as suddenly producing an unmentioned tape-recorder at the end of a detective story.) A scene littered with various species collapsing through giantism he would have accepted, but deliberate cheating he will not stand for.

'SPACE-OPERA' – A WILD RIOT

It is space-opera that is the wild riot of poisonous imaginings. Science-fiction proper is an exercise of the imagination within known limits, and can often be a severe test of logical thought. Postulate that Mars is arid, low in oxygen, has vegetation only in the *canali*, and free water only at the poles;[10] now your pioneer party has to enact its story within these conditions and their natural corollaries. They, and their consequences, have to be borne in mind with every move that is made. Or take Venus – long convention still allows you to assume that its surface is ninety-five per cent water, if you like; or you may adopt the more recent view that it is parched, and that the clouds that obscure it are of dust, but whichever you choose, you must continue consistently within your choice, for if you get a solecism past the editor, you certainly won't get it past all the readers. To obtain more variety than is offered by the much-explored solar system you are allowed to make use of an accepted convention variously named hyper-space, time-warp, et cetera, which gets you over the practical difficulties of travelling for light-years; but this hypothetical contraption *is* only a prop, it serves the same purpose as the programme which announces to an audience in London that the scene is a wood near Athens; once its job is done and you are in the neighbourhood of Sirius you are not absolved from treating the features of the district in a logical way – once you have decided what they are.

Contrary to the general impression, specifically juvenile science-fiction is rare. There is, of course, any amount of Dan Dare, Superman, and so on, in the space-opera class at various levels of publishing,[11] but when one has mentioned Robert Heinlein (*Space Cadet* Series, and others), Arthur C. Clarke (*The Sands of Mars*, and others), Angus MacVicar (*The Lost Planet* and *Return to the Lost Planet*), John Keir Cross (*The Angry Planet*, and others published in the U.S.A., but not here); David Duff's books; and the new series – *Martin Magnus* – which William Temple is now starting, the field of those who pay conscientious attention to cause and effect has been pretty well covered.[12]

One is told that the writing of such stories for juveniles is profitable since parents, feeling reassured by the classification, buy them, but that in practice boys themselves make little distinction between what is labelled juvenile, and what is not. As long as it is a good story that moves well they are little troubled by imperfect comprehension, being scarcely aware that it is imperfect. (I myself cannot imagine what I made of some parts of *The Time Machine* at the age of 12, but I remember, for all that, my great enthusiasm for it – and also that it gave me my first introductory inkling of the theory of evolution.)[13]

IS SCIENCE-FICTION ESCAPIST?

One has heard often enough that science-fiction is escapist. To a certain extent it is – and the house is an escape from natural discomforts, and civilisation is an escape from barbarism, and mathematics is escape from chaos, so that the use of a vogue-word to give an indefinite sense of taint conveys only that the speaker does not, or thinks he should not, care for some kinds of escape. Every simplification is an escape from complexity, and any work of fiction must present a picture that is simplified and selected in order to illuminate a particular part of a great complexity, and make it more comprehensible. The particular job which science-fiction sets itself is to put before the reader, in a suitable setting, the problems that would follow a hypothetical event: the author then does his best to work out the consequences. If his conclusions differ from those of his reader, so much the better, for he has at least fulfilled one of his objects – he has given the reader something to think about. The impression that the American invented science-fiction is erroneous. What they did was to attach a somewhat repulsive label to their preferred branch of it, wherefore one would mention a few books on various literary levels, all of which come within Mr. Crispin's definition, and, in the case of the first group, precede the concoction of the generic term: *After London*, by Richard Jefferies (1884); the Wells 'scientific romances'; Conan Doyle's *Lost World*, *Poison Belt*, and others; *The Hampdenshire Wonder*, by J. D. Beresford; *The Purple Cloud*, and others, by M. P. Shiel; *A Voyage to Arcturus*, by David Lindsay; *Back to Methuselah*, by Bernard Shaw; *R.U.R* and *War with the Newts*, by Karel Capek; *Brave New World*, by Aldous Huxley; *The Last Man*, by Alfred Noyes; *People of the Ruins*, by Edward Shanks, to take just a few. And then, later: *Last and First Men* and *Starmaker*, by Olaf Stapledon; *Ape and Essence*, by Aldous Huxley; and, as quite recent, lighter weights: *Player Piano*, by Kurt Vonnegut; *Childhood's End*, by Arthur Clarke; *Greener Than You Think*, and (very shortly) *Bring the Jubilee*, by Ward Moore.[14]

SCIENCE-FICTION MAGAZINES

The American-favoured type of short story makes its first appearance as a rule in a magazine, and three of these predominate. *Astounding Science-Fiction* has been going long enough to have achieved a quality that is somewhat esoteric for English readers, for the ground that has been covered already enables, and, indeed, requires, a story to dispense with much preliminary scene-setting, but the editor, John Campbell, Jr., is a science graduate with a sharp eye for errors of fact, and a firm way with the author who tries to cheat.[15] His magazine is the focus of the near-highbrow science-fiction cults (not unsimilar to the intellectual jazz cults) which exist in a number of American universities. In *Galaxy*, the editor, Horace Gold, aims at much the same level, but leans towards more emphasis on the story, preferring a little more flesh on its scientific bones.[16] *The Magazine of Fantasy and Science Fiction*, under Anthony Boucher, has the

APPENDIX

highest literary standard of the three, and, as its name indicates, has wider scope – it has a peculiar knack of resurrecting good stories that have somehow been forgotten.[17]

The best stories from these magazines invariably reappear in anthologies, and are most conveniently found over here in that form. Edmund Crispin's *Best S-F* (Faber) has already been mentioned. Representative reprints of American anthologies include: *Star Science Fiction* (Boardman); *The Second Astounding S-F Anthology* (Grayson); *Nine Tales of Space and Time* (Weidenfeld and Nicholson);[18] and some anthologies of stories by British authors are: *No Place Like Earth* (Boardman); *Gateway to Tomorrow* (Museum Press); *Best from New Worlds* (Boardman).[19]

The stories in these collections are uneven in quality, for the form, in spite of giving an impression that anything goes, is not an easy one to manipulate, but in nearly all of them there will be found that attempt to exploit an idea which is the distinguishing characteristic between science-fiction proper, and the raygun-packing super-cowboys and super-Indians of the wide open space-opera.

155

Appendix

NOTES

First Published in *The Preparatory School Review* (October 1955), 6–11. Reprinted with permission. 'Space Opera' was coined as sub-genre of Science Fiction in 1941. It typically contains adventures, melodramatic action and warfare. Wyndham saw this 'comic wild west stuff' (*Scientifiction*, April 1937) as typically American.

1 *I, Claudius* (1934) is a novel by Robert Graves set in the Roman Empire. *Forever Amber* (1944) is a romantic novel by Kathleen Winsor set in seventeenth-century England.

2 Edmund Crispin was the pen name of Bruce Montgomery, author of crime fiction and from 1955 to 1970 editor of the *Best SF* collections published by Faber, which played a role in establishing SF in Britain.

3 'Scientific Romance' was a term dating from the 1840s but mainly late nineteenth and early twentieth century to identify early SF; see Brian Stapleford, *Scientific Romance in Britain, 1890–1950* (London: Fourth Estate 1985).

4 Isaac Asimov (1920–1992) was an American biochemist and SF author, famous for his Robot and *Foundation* series. Arthur C. Clarke (1917–2008) was an early proponent of space travel, publishing *The Exploration of Space* in 1951. Wyndham had met him before the war and in 1954 both collaborated with John Carnell, editor of *New Worlds*, to give a talk on SF to the National Book League.

5 *Things to Come* was the 1936 film adaptation of H. G. Wells's *The Shape of Things to Come* (1933), produced by Alexander Korda, directed by William Cameron Menzies and scripted by Wells himself.

6 Davy Crockett (1786–1836) was a US politician and frontiersman, known in pop culture as 'King of the Wild Frontier' and the subject of a TV serial in 1954–1955.

7 Jules Verne (1828–1905) was recognized by Wyndham as a co-founder of SF centred on technology, which Wyndham saw as a strong American tradition.

APPENDIX

8   1925 probably refers to the date when Hugo Gernsback, editor of *Amazing Stories*, brought out the first book edition of his novel *Ralph 124C 41+*, which was packed with technological innovations.

9   *The Food of the Gods and How It Came to Earth* was a 1903 novel by H. G. Wells, described by him as a 'fantasia on the change of scale in human affairs' in his 1903 paper to the Fabian Society 'The Question of Scientific Administrative Areas in Relation to Municipal Undertakings.' An experimental substance increases the size of animals, wasps and humans, leading to hostility between the 'little people' and 'Children of the Food'.

10 The 'canali' were linear markings on the surface of Mars observed in 1881 by the Italian astronomer Schiaparelli, mis-translated as 'canals' and therefore supposed evidence of human life on that planet.

11 Dan Dare, 'Pilot of the Future', ran in the *Eagle* comic from 1950 to 1967. Superman was a superhuman hero first shown in the USA in 1938. Though born on the planet Krypton, his guardians on Earth gave him the name Clark Kent.

12 Robert Heinlein's 1948 novel *Space Cadet* describes the experiences of Matt Dodson, who becomes a member of the Interplanetary Patrol in the Solar System. Arthur C. Clarke's 1951 novel *The Sands of Mars* describes the experiences of Matt Gibson, an SF author, on that planet, where he discovers that his son is a trainee astronaut. Angus MacVicar was the Scottish author of the Lost Planet series, which began with *The Lost Planet* (1953) and *Return to the Lost Planet* (1954), and which concerns the construction of an atomic-powered spaceship and travel to the eponymous 'lost planet' Hesikos. The Scottish author John Keir Cross published his novel *The Angry Planet* in 1945, described on its dust wrapper as 'an authentic first-hand account of a journey to Mars'. In 1954 Cross adapted Wyndham's *The Kraken Wakes* for television. William F. Temple, a friend of Arthur C. Clarke and SF author, published *Planet Rover* in 1954 and *Martin Magnus on Venus* in 1955, both focusing on an interplanetary trouble-shooter.

13 H. G. Wells's *The Time Machine: An Invention* (1895) famously depicts a human future where society is divided between the childlike Eloi who live on the surface and the menial Morlocks who live underground and tend that society's machinery.

14 Richard Jefferies's *After London: or, Wild England* (1884) depicts a future where London has submerged and society has reverted to barbarism. Arthur Conan Doyle's *The Lost World* (1912) centres on the Amazon basin, while *The Poison Belt* (1913) describes attempts to confront a poisonous ether. Both centre on the scientist Professor Challenger. J. D. Beresford's *The Hampdenshire Wonder* (1911)

describes a child prodigy, perhaps partly modelled on H. G. Wells. M. P. Shiel, Montserrat-born, is remembered for his apocalyptic fiction, notably *The Purple Cloud* (1901, revised in the 1920s), where one Adam Jeffson discovers a deadly cloud in the Arctic which spreads gradually across Europe. It was described by Wells as 'brilliant' in *The Discovery of the Future* (1925). The Scottish author David Lindsay's *A Voyage to Arcturus* (1920) is set mainly on the fantasy planet Tormance and presents a complex symbolic sequence which has been seen as anticipating weird fiction. George Bernard Shaw's *Back to Methuselah* (1921) is a series of five plays with a broad period range introduced by an extensive preface and is a frequent reference point in Wyndham's writing. The Czech author Karel Capek's *War with the Newts* (1936) describes the discovery of intelligent newts and their subsequent conflict with humanity. Wyndham's 1937 review 'Revolt of the Animals' cited it as an example of the 'race suicide theme'. Capek's 1920 play *R.U.R.* (i.e. *Rossum's Universal Robots*) explores artificial factory workers. The poet Alfred Noyes's novel *The Last Man* (1940) describes how a death ray wipes out humanity. Edward Shanks's *The People of the Ruins* focuses on how a researcher in physics is accidentally frozen for 150 years and the future society he encounters. Olaf Stapledon's *Starmaker* (1937) describes a spiritual voyage and meetings with group minds which continues his exploration of historical cycles in *First and Last Men* (1930). Wyndham reviewed *Starmaker* in 1937. Aldous Huxley's *Ape and Essence* (1948) presents a framed film script describing a lapse into barbarism following an atomic war. Kurt Vonnegut's first novel *Player Piano* (1952) describes the extensive use of commercial automation in the wake of a third world war and subsequent industrial unrest. Arthur C. Clarke's 1953 novel *Childhood's End* describes the benign invasion of the Earth by the Overlords and the transformation of childhood through group minds. US author Ward Moore's *Greener Than You Think* (1947) describes the environmental disaster which follows the use of an untested spray which triggers uncontrolled growth in grasses. Wyndham reviewed the novel in 1949. Moore's *Bring the Jubilee* (1953) is an alternative history where the South wins the Civil War.

15 *Astounding Science Fiction* was a leading US magazine of SF. Founded in 1930, its editorship was taken over by John W. Campbell, who changed its title in 1960 to *Analog Science Fact & Fiction*.

16 The US magazine *Galaxy Science Fiction* began publication in 1950, edited by Horace Gold. Wyndham contributed to this and *Astounding*.

17 *The Magazine of Fantasy & Science Fiction* under Anthony Boucher's editorship began publication in 1949.

NOTES

18 Of the SF anthologies named by Wyndham, *Star Science Fiction* began its series in 1953, edited by Frederik Pohl. John W. Campbell edited *The Second Astounding Science-Fiction Anthology* in 1954. *Nine Tales of Space and Time* was edited by Raymond J. Healy in 1955. There were differences between the US and UK editions.

19 The final anthologies named were all edited by John Carnell. *No Place Like Earth* (1954) took its title from Wyndham's 1951 story, included here with 'Survival'. It also included an introduction by Arthur C. Clarke. *Gateway to Tomorrow* (1954) took as its opening story Wyndham's 'Dumb Martian'. *The Best from New Worlds Science Fiction* (1955) carried an introduction by Wyndham.

General Index

ABC TV 5
adaptations 5
A for Andromeda 5
After London 39, 107, 154, 157
Air Wonder Stories 8, 93
Alas Babylon 108
Aldiss, Brian 4, 6, 69, 72, 109, 112, 115, 116, 121, 122
Alfred Hitchcock Presents 122
Amazing Stories 2, 23, 74, 117, 119, 120, 121, 125
Amis, Kingsley 4, 5, 6, 109–111, 115, 124
Analog 125, 158
Anderson, Poul 111
A Pattern of Islands 121
Ape and Essence 44, 154, 158
Arata, Stephen 116
Argosy magazine 41, 82, 119
Ashley, Mike 116, 117
Asimov, Isaac 21, 105, 115, 148, 156
Astor, John Jacob 17
Astounding Science Fiction 107, 125, 158
Atwood, Margaret 6, 45, 60, 116, 119, 120
Australia 55, 56
Authentic Science Fiction Monthly 100–101, 123
A Voyage to Arcturus 154, 158
A Voyage to Puerilia 102

Back to Methuselah 47, 58, 120, 154, 158
Baker, Frank 95–96
Ballard, J. G. 4, 69, 72, 112–113, 115, 125
Balmer, Edward 13
BBC 4, 5, 59, 62, 115
Bedales School 1, 2, 7
Beresford, J. D. 20, 107, 124, 154, 157–158
Bergson, Henri 58
Best SF 78–79, 115, 121, 124, 147, 155
Binder, Eando 21
Binns, Amy 1, 57, 115, 117, 118, 120, 122
Black Mask 99
Boucher, Anthony 154–155, 158
Bova, Ben 120
Brackett, Leigh 40–41
Bradbury, Ray 73, 109, 115, 122, 124
Bradford, J. S. 122
Brave New World 20, 35, 65, 111, 154
Brazil 54–56
Bring the Jubilee 154, 158
Brooke, Rupert 52, 53
Brown, Fredric 122
Bruhm, Stephen 119
Brunner, John 72, 109, 112, 115

GENERAL INDEX

Bulmer, Kenneth 115
Burdekin, Katherine 103
Burroughs, Edgar Rice 13, 111
Burroughs, William 113
Butler, Octavia E. 46–47, 119
Butler, Samuel 112

Campbell, John W. 95, 154, 158, 159
Cape Canaveral 112
Capek, Karel 17, 94, 122, 154, 158
Carnell, John 4, 51, 69–70, 104, 113, 120, 124, 156, 159
Childhood's End 154, 158
Children of the Damned 49, 120
China 23–24
Christopher, John (Sam Youd) 34, 69, 112, 113, 115, 117, 118, 124
Churchill, Winston 27
Clark, Simon 118
Clarke, Arthur C. 52, 69, 79–80, 96, 105, 112, 113, 115, 120, 122, 148, 153, 154, 156, 157, 158, 159
cloning 35
Cold War 39–44, 51–52
Coleridge, Samuel Taylor 78
Collier, John 122
Collier's Magazine 3, 31, 82, 118, 122
Comstockery 101, 123
Conan Doyle, Arthur 154, 157
Confessions of an English Opium-Eater 78
Conklin, Groff 96
Creative Evolution 58
Crispin, Edmund 4, 78–79, 105, 115, 121, 124, 147, 154, 155, 156
Crockett, Davy 148, 156
Cross, John Keir 153, 157

Danse Macabre 116
Dare, Dan 153, 157
Darr House 120
Darwin, Charles 66–67

De Quincy, Thomas 78
Dianetics 79
Dickson, Paul 120
Discourses Biological and Geologica 119
Doctor Who 5
Downey, Adrian M. 119
Dr. Strangelove 53
Duff, David 153

Earth Abides 40
Ehrlich, Max 98
Eliot, T. S. 33
Etidorhpa 15
Even a Worm 122
Everybody's Weekly 82

Falkner, J. S. 125
Fantastic 4
Fantasy 22
Fantasy Awards 102
Fantasy Review 95–96, 117, 122–123
Fantasy and Science Fiction 125
FBI 101
Fearn, John Russell 117
Flood, Leslie 21
Forever Amber 147, 156
Fort, Charles 121
Four Quartets 33
Frank, Pat 109
Frankenstein 103
Fraser, Raymond 120
'Freedom of Space' 52

Galaxy Science Fiction 122, 125, 154, 158
Gallun, Raymond Z. 119
Gateway to Tomorrow 155, 159
Geddis, Norman Bel 77
Gernsback, Hugo 8, 9, 93, 99, 116, 157
Gillings, Walter H. 9, 72, 93, 94, 95, 101, 123
Gochenour, Phil 118

GENERAL INDEX

Gold, Horace 154, 158
Golding, William 122
Gould, Simon 118
Graves, Robert 121, 156
Greener Than You Think 30, 98,
 154, 158
Greenland, Colin 6
Grimble, Arthur 121

Hale, Arthur 120
Hamilton, Edmond 30
Hamlet 83
Hammond, John 121
Hansen, Solveig Lena 119
Harris, John Beynon (brother)
 1–2, 115
Hart, Derek 4, 119
Hays, Will H. 100, 101
H-bomb 107–109
Healey, Raymond J. 159
Heard, Gerald 96–97, 123
Heinlein, Robert 60, 153, 157
Henley, W. E. 64
Hiroshima 69, 113
Hodgson, William Hope 96
Hollywood 90
How the World Was One 120
Hoyle, Fred 5
Hubbard, L. Ron 79
Hubble, Nick 125
Hurst, L. J. 118
Huxley, Aldous 3, 20, 35, 44, 65,
 94, 96, 102, 111, 120, 154, 158
Huxley, Thomas Henry 46, 119

ICI 12, 13, 22
I, Claudius 121, 147, 156
Idiot's Delight, 53–54
'Inner-Space' 112, 125
International Science Fiction
 Convention (1951) 69–70
Interplanetary Flight 79
In the Days of the Comet 28
Invasion of the Sea 14
'Invictus' 64

Island of Doctor Moreau 7
It Can't Happen Here 28, 102

Japan 23–24, 30
Jefferies, Richard 39, 107, 154, 157
Jones, Raymond F. 123
'Joshua Fought the Battle' 81
Journey Beyond Tomorrow 110–111
Journey in Other Worlds 17

Ketterer, David 34, 73, 116, 117,
 118, 119
King Lear 122
King, Stephen 6, 116
Kipling, Rudyard 21
Kneale, Nigel 5, 111, 118–119
Korda, Alexander 156
Kornbluth, C. M. 72, 110
Krome, F. G. L. 119
'Kubla Khan' 78
Kuttner, Henry 43, 119

Lasser, David 8–9
Last and First Men 97, 154, 158
Latham, Rob 125
Level 7 108
Levin, Ira 35
Lewis, Sinclair 28, 102
Ley, Willy 79
Lilith's Brood trilogy 119
Lindsay, David 154, 158
Liverpool University 6
Lloyd, John Uri 15
Lollobrigida, Gina 90
London Underground 84
Loos, Anita 98
Lost on Venus 13
Luckhurst, Roger 30–31, 125
Lysenko, Trofim 28

Maatta, Jerry 118
Machen, Arthur 96, 123
Mackintosh, F. H. 119
MacVicar, Angus 153, 157
Maine, Charles Eric 110

163

GENERAL INDEX

Manlove, C. N. 118
Manning, Laurence 30
Man and Superman 118, 122
Mars 15–16, 17–20, 54–55, 73–74, 78, 79, 122, 157
Martin Magnus on Venus 153, 157
Marvel Science Stories 79
Matthews, Graham, J. 118
McCarthyism 41, 10
Mengele, Josef 35
Men Like Gods 64–65
Menzies, William Cameron 156
Merril, Judith 72, 79
Metropolis 18
MGM 49
Michael Joseph 110–111
Might is Right 116
Miller, Alistair 120
Miller, P. Schuyler 112, 125
Mind at the End of Its Tether 97
Ministry of Information 25
Mitchell, Gladys 116
'Monsters May Be Real!' 39–40, 119
Montgomery, Bruce 78
Moorcock, Michael 69, 104, 112–113, 125
Moore, Ward 3, 30, 97, 154, 158
Morris, William 112
Mr. Allenby Loses the Way 96
Munchausen, Baron 100
Murray, Andy 119
Mutant 43, 119
mutants 42–44
My Fair Lady 90

Nakaa (Maori) 65
Nazis 23, 24–25, 32, 34–36, 41
Nebula 125
'Next Step the Moon' 52
New Caledonia 56
New Maps of Hell 109–111, 124
New Wave 112–113
New Worlds 4, 51–52, 69–72, 100, 103–105, 120, 121, 125

New Writings in SF 115
Nine Tales of Space and Time 155, 159
Nineteen Eighty-Four 32, 41, 71, 102, 111
No Place Like Earth 155, 159
Noyes, Alfred 154, 158

Odd John 20
ODESSA network 35
Oliver-Hobley, Christie 120, 121
On the Beach 55
Opel, Fritz von 14
Oppenheimer, J. Robert 53, 65
Orwell, George 32, 41, 71, 102, 111
Out of the Unknown 5
Out of This World 5

Paris Review 120
Peake, Mervyn 122
Pearl Harbor 38
Penn Club 1, 2
People of the Ruins 154
Phillips, Peter 52
Pirates of Venus 13
Planet Rover 157
Player Piano 102, 154, 158
Pohl, Frederik 3, 110, 115, 159
Pollard, Neil 119
Princeton University 5, 110
Priyadarsini, Pretty 119
Production Code (1930) 100
Proverbs (Bible) 86
Publishers Weekly 120
Pygmalion 90

Quatermass 5, 111, 125
Quatermass II 125
Quatermass and the Pit 125

Radcliffe, Garnett 97–98
Radio Times 125
Raisborough, Jayne 120
Ralph 124C 41+ 93, 157

GENERAL INDEX

Realm of Perhaps 4
Redbeard, Ragnar 116
Rees, Amanda 116
Return to the Islands 121
Return to the Lost Planet 153, 157
Rice, Elmer 102
Rilla, Wolf 119
robots 21, 103
Roshwald, Mordecai 108
Royal Corps of Signals 25
Ruddick, Nicholas 118
R.U.R. 154, 158
Russell, Eric Frank 72, 93–94,
    112, 117, 121, 122, 124
Russia 18–19

Sawyer, Andy 116, 119, 120, 123
Schiaparelli, Giovanni 157
Science Fantasy 72, 101, 123
Science Fiction Convention (1957)
    4
'Science Fiction and the Space
    Age' 120
Scientific Romance 148, 156
Scientific Romance in Britain 156
Scientifiction 9, 93, 94, 116, 122
'Seeds from Space' 30
Seidel, Matthew James 119
Senate House (University of
    London) 32
Shadow on the Hearth 79
Shanks, Edward 107, 124, 154,
    158
Shaw, George Bernard 47, 58, 90,
    112, 118, 120, 122, 154, 158
Sheckley, Robert 110–111
Shelley, Percy Bysshe 64
Sherwood, Robert E. 53–54
Shiel, M. P. 154, 158
Shute, Nevil 55
Sirius 152
Sky TV 46
Smith, Denis 119
Smith, Grover 120
Smith, Thorne 98

Smith's Trade News 123
Soviet Union 28, 37, 48, 51–52, 54,
    59, 98
'Space Age, Year One' 51
Space Cadet series 153, 157
'Space-Opera' 105, 152–153, 156
Space Race 113
'Special Delivery' 52
Spenser, Edmund 8, 85
Sprigg, T. Stanhope 117
Sputnik 51–52, 120
Stapledon, Olaf 20, 94, 97, 154,
    158
Stapleford, Brian 156
Starmaker 154, 158
Star Science Fiction 155, 159
Startling Stories 81
Stewart, George R. 40
Stock, Adam 118, 119
Superman 153, 157
Swastika Night 102

Tales from the White Hart 115
Tales of Wonder 95, 98, 117, 122,
    123
Temple, William F. 153, 157
Tennyson, Alfred Lord 36, 37
Tevis, Walter 111
The Age of the Triffids 118
The Angry Planet 153, 157
The Author 124
The Best from New Worlds 155, 159
The Big Eye 98
The Black Flame 98–99
The Boys from Brazil 35
The Brink 109
The Canopy of Time 109
'The Country of the Blind' 28
The Death of Grass 34, 118
The Discovery of the Future 158
The Exploration of Space 79, 156
The Faerie Queen 85
The First Men in the Moon 99,
    112
The Flames: A Fantasy 97

165

GENERAL INDEX

The Food of the Gods 107, 112, 151–152, 157
The Great Fog 123
The Hampdenshire Wonder 20, 107, 154, 157–158
The House on the Borderland 96
The Invasion of the Body Snatchers 60
The Island of Doctor Moreau 85, 93
'The Jolly Company' 52
'The Kraken' 36, 37
The Lady from Venus 97–98
The Land of the Triffids 118
The Last Man 154, 158
The Listener 107, 124
The Long Tomorrow 40–41
The Lost Planet 153, 157
The Lost World 154, 157
'The Lunar Chrysalis' 119
The Magazine of Fantasy and Science Fiction 154–155, 158
The Man Who Fell to Earth 111
'The Man of the Year Million' 10, 116
The Martian Chronicles 73
The Night of the Triffids 118
The Other Side of the Sky 120
The Passing Show 13, 15, 117
The People of the Ruins 107, 158
The Perversity of Things: Hugo Gernsback on Media 116
'The Plant Revolt' 30
The Poison Belt 154, 157
The Puppet Masters 60
The Purple Cloud 154, 158
The Quatermass Experiment 125
The Sands of Mars 79, 122, 153, 157
The Second Astounding S-F Anthology 155, 159
The Shape of Things to Come 29, 156
The Space Merchants 110
The Tempest 64
The Time Machine 14, 17, 116, 157

The Time Machines (Ashley) 116
'The Valley of Spiders' 66
The Voyage of the Beagle 67
The War of the Worlds 18, 31, 49
The Year of the Comet 117
Things to Come 148, 156
Tisdall, Laura 46, 119
'To the Cuckoo' 61
Tolkien, J. R. R. 111
TV Times 124
Twain, Mark 77
Twilight World 110

VanderMeer, Jeff 6, 116
Venus 11, 12, 13, 22, 31, 56, 70, 97, 105, 109
Verne, Jules 14, 103, 105–106, 108, 149, 150, 156
Village of the Damned 5, 48, 120
Vonnegut, Kurt 3, 102, 154, 158

Wagner, Thomas M. 119
Walton, Jo 118
War with the Newts 154, 158
Watkins, Susan 120
'Wayback Machine' 121
Weinbaum, Stanley G. 95, 98–99
Wells, H. G. 1, 7, 9, 10, 14, 17, 18, 19, 25, 28, 29, 31, 49, 52, 64–65, 66, 73, 85, 89, 93, 94, 97, 99–100, 103, 105, 107, 108, 109, 112, 116, 121, 123, 124, 148, 151, 154, 156, 157–158
Wembridge, Eleanor Rowland 123
When the Sleeper Wakes 10, 19
When Worlds Collide 13
Whitbourn, John 118
White Horse pub 115
Wickes, George 120
Williamson, Jack 79
Wilson, Grace (partner/wife) 2
Winsor, Kathleen 156
Woman's Journal 82, 84

GENERAL INDEX

Wonder Stories 8, 11, 30, 116
Wonder Stories Quarterly 20
Wordsworth, William 61
World Without Men 110
World's Fair 77

Wylie, Philip 13
Wymer, Roland 41, 119

xenogenesis 46–47
Xenogenesis Trilogy 46–47

Index to Wyndham's Works

'A Life Postponed' 90–91
'...And Other Expositions' 96, 123
'And the Green Grass Grew...' 98, 123
'And the Walls Came Tumbling Down...' 81–82

Best from 'New Worlds' 103–104
'Beyond the Screen' 22, 25

'Child of Power' 19
Chocky **59–63,** 120–121
'Chronoclasm' 73
'Consider Her Ways' 5, 85–87, 110, 122
Consider Her Ways **69–91**, **122**

'Derelict of Space' 24–25
'Did Mr. Baker Lose His Way?' 96
'Dumb Martian' 5, 78
'Doomsday in Moronia' 98, 123

'Exiles on Asperus,' 20–21

'Future Flying Fiction' 93

'Has Science Fiction a Future?' 111–112, 125
'He's Converting the Masses' 94, 122

'How Do I Do?' 83

'Invisible Monster' 12

Jizzle 82–84, 122
'Jizzle' 82–83, 122
'John Wyndham on Science Fiction' 6, 106, 110–112, 124, 125
'Judson's Annihilator' 22–23, 25, 117

'*Mars*: A.D. 2094' 54–55
'Meteor' 74–75
Midwich Main 49
'Monsters May Be Real!' 40, 119
Much Abides 40

'No Place Like Earth' 5
'No Science Fiction This' 103, 107–108, 124
'Not So Simple' 100–101, 124

'Odd' 87–88
'Oh, Where, Now, is Peggy MacRafferty?' 90
'Operation Peep' 72, 77, 121
'Opposite Number' 77–78
'Opposite Numbers' 77
Out of the Deeps 3, 38

'Pawley's Peepholes' 72, 76–77
'Perforce to Dream' 83–84

168

'Personally Speaking' 52
'Phoney Meteor' 74, 75–76
Planet Plane 16
Plan for Chaos **34–36**, 119

'Random Quest' 89–90
Re-Birth 3, 41
'Reservation Deferred' 84
'Revolt of the Animals' 94
'Roar of Rockets!' 102–103, 124

'Satirical Salad' 97, 123
'Science Fiction' 108–109, 124
'Science-Fiction: Space-Opera' 2,
    8, 104–107, 124, **147–155**
'Science Fiction: The Facts' 103,
    124
'Slave to the Fantastic' 95–96, 123
Sleepers of Mars 19, 116, 117
'Sowing New Thoughts' 98, 123
'Stitch in Time' 88
Stowaway to Mars 15–19, 94
'Survival' 72–73

'Technical Slip' 83
The Best from 'New Worlds' 4,
    71–72, 124
*The Best of John Wyndham:
    1932–1949* 117
*The Best of John Wyndham:
    1951–1960* 122
The Chrysalids 3, 4, **39–45,** 119
The Curse of the Burdens 2
The Day of the Triffids 3, 4, 13,
    27–34, 35, 45
'The Emptiness of Space' 56–57
'The Fate of the First Men' 96–97,
    123
'The Flame That Went Out' 98,
    123
'The Incomplete Machen' 96, 123

The Kraken Wakes 3, 4, **36–39**, 45
'The Living Lies' 70–71, 105, 121
'The Lost Machine' 15–16, 21–22
'The Man from Beyond' 22
'The Man from Earth' 12
The Midwich Cuckoos 5, 20, **45–49**,
    61
'The Moon. A.D. 2044' 53–54
The Outward Urge 3, **51–57**
'The Pattern of Science Fiction'
    77, 101–102, 122, 124
'The Perfect Creature' 7–8, 118
'The Puff-Ball Menace' 13, 30
'The Red Stuff' 79–81
'The Revolt of the Triffids' 31,
    118
'The Scientific Novel' 103, 124
The Secret People 10–11, 13–15,
    94
The Seeds of Time 4, 121–122
'The Third Vibrator' 12
'The Trojan Beam' 23–24
'The Venus Adventure' 11
'Time to Rest' 5, 73–74
Trouble with Lichen 3, 6, **57–63**

'Una' 79, 118, 122

'Venus: A.D. 2144' 56
'Vivisection' 7

Wanderers of Time 11–12, 117, 118
Web **63–68**
'Why This Cosmic Wild West
    Stuff?' 9, 94–95
'Why Blame Wells?' 22, 99–100,
    123
'Will This Hasten the Death
    of the Detective Thriller?'
    102–103, 124
'Worlds to Barter' 9–10

www.ingramcontent.com/pod-product-compliance
Lightning Source LLC
LaVergne TN
LVHW010720180925
821343LV00003B/55